The Long Game

Short Writings On Ideas That Last

Jerry G. Banks

The Long Game: Short Writings About Ideas That Last

Copyright © 2026 by Jerry G. Banks

First published in the USA in 2026 by Story Gold Media, Denver, Colorado

ISBN 979-8-234-01905-9 Hardback

ISBN 979-8-9989839-7-9 Paperback

ISBN 979-8-9989839-8-6 eBook

Library of Congress Control Number: 2026905781

Editor

James Thole, storygoldmedia.com

Cover Design

Jack Banks Green

Interior Design

Story Gold Media

Portrait Photographer

Cindy Maurer, C's Photography, csphotographystudio.com

To the seven problems known as my grandchildren.

Jack, Julia, Charlie, Brenden, Evie, Nora and Hazel.

Thank you for the love and joy you have brought to my life.

I love you with all my heart!

Grandpa

Table of Contents

Part Five
Essays

Preface

I was born and raised in Glenwood, a small southwest Iowa town of about 4,000 to 5,000 population. It was much like growing up in Mayberry RFD or in a Leave It to Beaver neighborhood. As I look back on it now, I'm so thankful for my experiences, memories, teachers, parents, neighbors, mentors, friends, and classmates from my youth. There is no question that they all were like ingredients to the recipe called me. But also were my genetics. I came from a long line of German-Irish entrepreneurs and very independent thinkers. One of my grandfathers from way back was one of the youngest enlisted drummer boys of the Revolutionary War at the incredible age of thirteen. His father brought him and his siblings by ship across the Atlantic in the mid-1700s on the ship christened "Hope".

My great-grandfather Charley Overturf was a blacksmith in central Iowa and at some point lost his hand. Rather than finding a new career as, say, a librarian or barkeep, Charley invented attachments to his stub arm to allow him to continue in his trade. He also had numerous inventions that he obtained patents on. One of his many inventions was a mobile cement mixer pulled by a team of horses.

Another invention was a collapsible mold used to create culverts under streets and then reuse the mold. I think I know where our family's genetic traits of creativity, resilience, and stubbornness come from.

His daughter (my grandmother) married my grandfather Harry Banks. Harry was also an inventor of numerous items that also were awarded patents. I'm guessing that his father-in-law Charley was an influence and advisor in Harry's creative nature. One of Harry's inventions (first electric tabletop potato peeler) was the genesis of today's high-volume vegetable peelers used by potato chip factories around the world. Someone once said that if someone in the world eats a potato chip, its production is related all the way to my grandfather. Unfortunately, my grandparents sold their interest in the patent in the early 1960s for $25,000 when they retired and moved to Florida. Harry had other inventions such as an oil burner for stoves and a mileage dial that could tell you what roads to take and how many miles it would be to get from point A to point B. The mileage dial was the early and mechanical version of MapQuest or Google Maps in my mind.

In my view, the result of both my genetics and my school-age years and most likely a lot of other factors too, I have become a very creative yet reflective person. I find the combination of creativity and reflectiveness can have its positives and negatives. On one hand I question almost everything, research much, and then reflect upon my findings, and generally see how the findings fit into my life or how I can use the information. All this is good. On the other hand, I also at times way-overthink or overanalyze whatever subject or topic has caught my attention. I also blame this concoction on being part of the cause of my tendency to be a daydreamer. I daydream about the future or about certain subjects, situations, or relationships, which in turn create almost mental videos or vignettes of what my life might be like if my daydreams came to fruition. I believe that all humans have an internal self-fulfilling prophecy compass embedded within them. As I wrote in my first book (Eat Sh*t and Smile), I refer to it as our internal GPS. This internal GPS has the power to turn dreams into reality.

As an example, in 2004, I penned a small piece that goes like this:

A good friend.

A big porch.

A big fireplace.

A barn.

An old dog.

A good horse.

A tractor.

An old truck.

A place to fish.

A tree to cut.

A sunrise view.

A good cup of coffee.

Somewhere to go.

Something to do.

Someone to love.

These are my dreams.

These are my goals.

It was handwritten on a piece of blue notebook paper and put away in the back of a file. In 2017, I was cleaning out some old files and came across the piece. I had totally forgotten about it and was quite taken aback by what I had written. I hadn't seen or even remembered it for thirteen-plus years. What's crazy is that in 2010, six years after writing the piece, bought an acreage with 90 acres, 3 ponds, some outbuildings including a turn-of-the-century barn. In 2013, I built a house on that farm. One with a sunrise view, a big fireplace, and two big porches. I had an old truck and a tractor and one of my favorite things to do was to cut firewood. The cover of this book is a photo of the driveway one snowy Sunday and many of the pieces contained herein were written at what our family lovingly calls "The Farm".

So, how did I get started writing? Unintentionally, it started with a poem. As I recall, I did not think to myself "Hey Jerry— why don't you write a poem!" I had never been, nor am I today, an avid reader of poetry. I think the attraction to poetry, given my reflective nature, was because it to me is so lyrical. Much like a lyric to a song. I love music even though I personally can't carry a tune in a bucket. My primary attraction to music is not so much the tune or beat as it is the lyrics. I prefer and enjoy songs that have meaning and/or metaphors contained in the lyrics that touch me or mean something to me. Thus, I'm guessing my writing took on an almost musical quality where there was a beat or cadence to speaking it and it had to be rhythmic for me to like it. That's the best I can come up with as to why poetry was my chosen form of writing. And perhaps it chose me versus me choosing it!

What brought about my writing is perhaps simpler to explain but far more deeply personal. In the fall of 1994 my wife of eighteen years told me she wanted a divorce. Thankfully for all, I won't go into the gory details of it but let's just leave it to say that it was an incredibly emotional time for me.

One night after being ejected from my house and family, I found myself on the leatherette piece of crap couch I had borrowed from my parents' basement. It would help fill the living room of the rental house I was now forced to live in. I had a pad of paper and a pen and

I had intended to make notes about something. Such as what needed to be done the next day, or things I needed to do at work, or what was going on in the divorce. But for some odd reason my mind was stuck on another subject. And a weird one at that!

My mind was stuck on why some people are picky and why some people are not picky. As I thought about the subject my reflective nature kicked in about the application of the question to me. Was I picky? Or not picky? I started thinking about food, wine, and other things and decided that I can be picky, a little bit, but I'm not over the top with it. I like what I like and know what I like. On the other hand, other people are far less so and will take about anything on the menu.

So, then it leads me to the next thought process. Is knowing what you like and pursuing your likes a bad thing or a negative trait? Do others view my nature to know what I like or don't like as being too over-the-top negative or do they perceive me as one who has good taste? Do you see that reflective part of me as mentioned earlier? I picked up my pad and paper and just started writing. The following came out of nowhere. I spent perhaps ten minutes on it and have never changed a word of it since. Here goes!

The Pursuit of Preferences

(May 1995)

There are some things in this life,

for which I take particular joy.

Upon this narrow subject, my thoughts I wish to deploy.

For the preferences of each individual,

defines the essence of their very being.

An evolving and growing state,

from which one's spirit should not be fleeing.

For if the state of these individual preferences

grows in definition and becomes more refined.

The quality of the life for which we live

Becomes greater in meaning and more defined.

In the alternative, however, I find.

That should the choices become more vague,

less discerning, ever less caring.

Then our mental vitality begins to lag.

Declining importance of personal choice

negates the value of one's very self.

For as your tastes grow more pliable,

care for your own happiness you put to shelf.

This is not to discourage a flexible personality.

But to encourage pursuit of one's personal tastes.

To refine them and define them with care.

And to dedicate to them time which not to waste.

The preferences for which I choose include:

fine cigars, I love a good smoke.

A great red wine or a vintage port perhaps.

The laughter that erupts from a new joke.

The tender bite of flavor from the spring lamb.

The mystery that stirs within the novel.

The love of my kids at which I marvel.

The closing of a deal I have pursued.

Or the simple time I share with a good friend.

To all of these I shall commit more time.

And to their greater enjoyment I shall ascend.

That was the very beginning. The thoughts, reflection, and emotions spilled out from there. I began writing and that night along with a few nights thereafter emotions came forth like a dam had broken. Most of the early writings were about the divorce, my kids, and so on. Many of those early ones, especially about the divorce and my emotional state at the time, have not been included in this book. Some early pieces relative to my kids or family are.

Now years later I find myself still writing. Over the years my writing has taken different forms and expanded my thinking. Sometimes still emotional, sometimes thankfully not. But they always tend to be reflective or introspective. I get something on my mind and it dwells and seems to swell there until I feel that the only way I can settle this, or be able to get to sleep that night, is if I write it down. Sometimes it is on a piece of paper, sometimes it is on the computer. It seems as though it is akin to unloading a dangerous weapon— my mind.

I once wrote a piece that addresses my *"Why Write?"* Let me end by sharing it with you now.

Pen on Paper

It brings study to my reasoning.

It lays down evidence to my dreams.

It provides courage to face my challenges.

It gives peace to smooth my anxiety.

It charts the pathways of my thoughts.

It gives voice to my heart.

It unloads the burdens on my mind.

It is my pen on paper.

Part One

Nature & Spirituality

I learn more about myself in reflection than I do during most any experience. Maybe what makes me different is that I often write about that reflection process and what comes from it.

The writings in this section date back to 1995 and come from two places that have always stirred something in me: airplanes and the outdoors. I've always enjoyed flying as a passenger—there's something about being suspended between earth and sky that opens up space for contemplation. Especially, at night, if the sky is clear I feel as though I'm flying between two galactic blankets; the stars above and the city lights below. "One Single Light," "One Can't Help But Believe," "The Jagged Edge," and "Airplanes" all came from those flights.

But most of my spiritual writings were born outdoors. From age thirteen to seventeen, I spent hours horseback riding across 600 acres near my hometown. In my adult life, I've lived on acreages and farms at different times. The most meaningful was a 255-acre farm where I spent twelve years—the most productive and spiritual period of my writing life. "Come Sunday," "Smoke Signals," "Seasons of the

Mind," and "Mankind" all came from that place. Working the land, cutting firewood, watching the seasons change—that's where I found God most clearly.

I'm a spiritual person with a strong belief in God, though I don't pretend to have all the answers or preach one path over another. I have faith in the goodness of people, faith in nature, and faith in something beyond what science can explain. I've studied Native American spirituality and found deep commonalities in their nature-based beliefs. After several experiences where facts and science couldn't explain what happened, I fell to acceptance. I call that acceptance Faith.

These writings reflect that journey.

Come Sunday

Come Sunday thousands will file into steepled buildings built by man, paid for by man, and nod in agreement to lectures given by man.

They will say it is the Word of God coming from a man of God, given to all in a House of God.

This is good, all is well, and as it has been for thousands of years.

But for me, come Sunday, I will stay on my farm and think of it as my church.

The pew is a seat on the dock of the pond.

The apostles speak to me through the sights and sounds of nature.

God's true Sun rises in the east and shines dawn's light upon all.

Trees rise and wave in jubilation and praise.

The prairie grass and bushes hum like an organ as the wind passes through their pipes.

Like stained glass panes; corn flowers, green and crimson leaves, black-eyed susans or yellow sunflowers fling color all about.

Birds sing soprano, frogs alto and bass.

Silently, I give gratitude for my blessings and offer true reverence for the miracles of nature.

Come Sunday, I may be missing the Word of God.

But, come Sunday I believe I will be experiencing the truth and reality of God.

And this is also good and well, and as it shall remain, come Sunday.

Smoke Signals

I cut firewood late this afternoon. It is a cold, brisk, overcast day here at the farm.

I jump in the gator and ride the trails to find a ready and down candidate for cutting.

The fresh air and brisk wind on my face are exhilarating. The burn in my fingers reminds me that I had frostbite once in my twenties from just such an expedition and I quickly find my gloves.

It doesn't take long to come across a down silver maple that once stood on one of the highest terraces here on the farm. I am certain the birds that once sat in this tree enjoyed the view over the ponds and valley below.

When I finish cutting and start loading, I am blessed with the sight of twelve deer running through the field below. I'm guessing they don't appreciate the sound of my chain saw and are seeking solitude. I wholeheartedly concur and silently apologize for disrupting their day.

Today's load just happens to be the fuel for tonight's burn. This is not always the situation. I have a ready cut volume of firewood in the barn in case of need or laziness. But today's cut is dead and dry, so I will just take it directly to the house.

With the load now stacked neatly under the cover of my porch, I proceed to go inside. I pour myself a glass of whiskey on ice. After a small sip or two I build a fire in my living room fireplace before landing on the couch to watch tonight's football game.

I have an hour before kick-off, so I turn the stereo on to listen to music. A shuffle mix of my favorite tunes, which include everything from country, to blues, to rock, to classical. Add in a bit of Spanish guitar, some R&B. and oh yeah, don't forget my Reggae tunes.

Only to myself, I recognize my musical tastes are synonymous with my brain: a tangled-up mess.

As I listen to the music and sip on my honey-infused Jack Daniel's, I gaze at the fire and feel the warmth it radiates to my feet. I'm thinking to myself that those logs now burning were lying motionless in the field just a few hours earlier. The fire's glow is mesmerizing, the warmth appreciated, and the scent enjoyed.

I think of the years that tree stood like a soldier overlooking the valley below. It started as a seed and took years to grow. Through the years, I think of the storms it endured, the sun and water it absorbed, the shade it provided. How many birds spent their childhood in a nest within my tree or had their first flight from one of its branches? And now, with each burn, the tree will be gone and up in smoke. It almost saddens me to think of that tree's life span over decades, all to be gone in a few hours due to my desire for a fire just to warm my toes and provide a dreamy scene. I also wonder: *How much whiskey have I drunk?*

But then it occurs to me that perhaps these burning logs are simply telling their story. A story of the transition of life. Ashes to ashes, dust to dust.

I hope and believe God is watching as both the tree and I join together to send smoke signals through tonight's starlit sky. Smoke signals sending gratitude His way for the wonders of nature, the blessings of life, and the joy He has given to both this tree and me. All occurred upon a small piece of dirt, high upon an Iowa hillside.

Ashes to Ashes, Dust to Dust.

Smoke Signals to God from the tree and me.

My Friend, My Therapist, My Counselor

For once this week my mind isn't thinking about today's done list or tomorrow's to-do list.

It isn't thinking about who did this or that done why—the things that always seem to clutter my mind.

Relaxed beside my fire pit, finally, I'm freed from analysis of the chess game we all call life.

For an hour or two this evening, this weary brain is only tracing fleeing sparks, embers aglow, and the path of rising billows outward bound.

The scent of the air quiets the pathway to this beloved state of mind, as iced-down whisky soothes the bumps and lumps within my body and soul.

I relish the warmth freely given by you, my friend, as my shoeless feet rest upon your boulder-bound fire.

Crackles, snaps and pops of the burn harmonize with owls, crickets and coyotes to give a gentle melody to your dancing flames.

Just like the swing of a golden watch can lead one into a trance, the mind can cleanse when tired eyes get lost in the glow of wood upon wood all afire.

As I end another night's session, I give gratitude for your warmth, your kind and healing way. Yet all you ask of me is another piece of elm or oak to feed your hungry burn.

Oh, fire pit, dear fire pit, you are my friend, my therapist, my counselor; you bring me warmth and you bring me peace.

Harvest Time

Fall is without doubt, my most favorite time of the year here in the Midwest. If you want to experience the soundless brag and boast of the hillsides take an October drive along the scenic highways of Western Iowa or Eastern Nebraska. The palette of color jumps off nature's canvas and silently speaks of beauty, nature, peace, and joyful reflections of the past.

As you journey either side of the Missouri River, take stock of the uniform rows of corn and beans that are laid like a quilt between the valleys and hillsides. Soon farmers will be harvesting the soldier-like crops that were born of simple seeds planted in the soil just a few months ago.

The farmers' sweat, the tractors' pull, nature's sun, and God's rain have come together to hopefully fill the wagons, train cars and grain bins that dot America's heartland.

Storms struck, thunder roared, rain fell or didn't, and blistering sunshine were all encountered for yet another season. Some plants were destroyed, and others bypassed with a nod of luck and forgiveness. And such is the life of the farmer. Hard work, God's smile or wreck, a little luck and maybe just maybe the bounty they hoped for will be realized and appreciated.

Much like a farmer's season, our individual lives follow a similar but expanded track. The season is not a few months. For most, it is year stacked upon year until God's picker decides it's time for our homecoming harvest. For some, it comes early and too soon. For others, perhaps not soon enough.

Exercising the gift of maturity, time and reflection I can now see that I won the lottery by being planted in the best human growth soil the world has to offer, the United States of America. Some incredible folks that I call parents nurtured me from seed to maturity. They did their best to protect me from the storms and help to direct me in finding my way. More than once, I fought them and had to realize my own path, a harder path, a tumultuous path at times. I live in gratitude for my home soil, my loving parents, and my unique path. My scenic path included experiences of discovery, challenges, educating failures, humiliating losses and life changing opportunities as I travelled the uncharted thoroughfare of life. Since it was my life, it also had to be my path.

I'm not ready to be harvested quite yet. I'm still growing, more so in reflection, understanding and yes maybe even a notch or two in the belt. I'm going to fight the picker's call and I hope to withstand the storms when the doctors call. I have a vision for the path that lies in front of me and as before, it enthusiastically beckons me forward. Just as it always has been, it always shall be, my uniquely crafted path.

But now, slightly different than in the past, I now possess the desire, wisdom and power to slow down and enjoy the scenic view, taste the rewards, appreciate the sweet gift of life and the beauty of the harvest that lies along the path.

Harvest time is a beautiful time of year in the Midwest worthy of a long, slow drive along a scenic highway. Harvest is also a beautiful time of life, and it too is worthy of a long, enjoyable journey. Give gratitude and love your harvest. Appreciate your unique path just as I shall mine.

Harvest will end, and leaves will fall. Soon the cold of winter will set in, and another fall season will have settled to finality. The beauty of the golden leaves will be replaced with the golden flames of logs afire that warm the heart. And someday, so shall our harvest end. God willing, may we be filled with golden memories to comfort and warm our hearts as we fall like leaves to the ground.

Mankind

Mankind differs from the remainder of all known life. These differences provide us more responsibility than they do superiority. But in this sense of responsibility, we need to humbly accept our superiority.

Like no other, Mankind has an innate ability to organize and train other species, to communicate in multiple methods, and the ability to invent. Human beings have the ability to discover, utilize and even manipulate resources in infinite combinations and for infinite reasons. Such as for business, art, science, religion and education. No other species has such capabilities.

As such, I believe, God intended mankind to be in somewhat of a leadership role. Sadly, however, throughout history and yet today, we have at times failed or made errors in our position. Our learning process is slow but never-ending, always challenging and always in flux. We make mistakes. We learn. We change. We adapt.

Our leadership is further complicated and challenged by our lack of unity. We have no common voice and are always at some level of disagreement. We are more of a committee of committees, leading our own, some of whom are listening at times, some of whom are not, and most in the middle, lost but intending well.

Yes, Mankind has and will continue to make mistakes. Thankfully God provided us an earth, a universe and an environment that is more resilient and self-healing than I think we realize at times. He provided for our blunders and foresaw our weaknesses.

We were intended to lead and to marshal the species and resources created by God in his grand experiment. And that we should continue to do, all in pursuit of that which is right and just for the long term. I know not the outcome or the purpose, but I am confident in God's will and appointment.

Our challenge should be to test our actions, our motives, our theories and ask ourselves "As God's chosen leaders are we serving God's best interest and purpose?"

Seasons of the Mind

Our mind is like the weather I think. Full of change and seasons and moods of sorts.

A mind can be as free as the wind and as wild as the lightning-lit sky.

It can feel as light as dawn and as clear and new as the morning's fresh dew.

It can rain gloom like never-ending monsoons or feel as frigid as the arctic blast.

A mind can feel spiteful as the tornado that rips and roars and as angry as the mighty storm at sea.

The mind can live in a haze as thick as the morning fog or be blinded by a driving snow.

It can cast hurt like a summer storm and yell displeasure as thunder upon the crowds.

The mind can spread the warmth of the heart like the sun on the desert floor and it can breathe happiness like a spring day does upon a mountain meadow.

Ah, but lest we forget, while only God controls the weather, we are empowered to direct our minds to their daily result.

Tis ours to choose our own temperate display each and every day.

Forces Within

Evil events and negative forces have left scars upon my memory and soul.

They are always there, typically to the back. Sometimes speaking to me and trying at times to drive my mind or distract me from my course.

But with belief in God, spiritual guidance, love from my friends and family, and an internal compass directing me towards positive dreams and positive outcomes, they stay to the back and their volume is kept low.

When these scars try to rise again and come to the front of my mind, I recognize them for who they are and where they belong. They are the forces that once derailed me from my goals, my happiness and my peace. They occurred in the past and the past is where they belong.

It's okay to see them from a distance now and again, and to recall their transgressions from time to time.

But I also live in acceptance that they no longer define me, drive me, or control me.

Intrinsic positivity is the driving force of this life now and forevermore.

Super Bloom!

T he first spring after a forest fire roars through, a phenomenon occurs in nature referred to by foresters as the "Super Bloom."

New growth generously and abundantly occurs with new plants, trees and flowers. The new growth doesn't let the fear of another fire prevent them from taking a risk to grow again. They bloom and grow regardless of the risk of another fire. So it should be with our hearts and our lives when risks we take go down in flames. We need to let the Super Bloom occur within us, in spite of our fear of getting burnt again.

Sometimes when you take risks you get burnt. Getting burnt can harden the heart, the outlook, and the enthusiasm for risk taking. Lessons learned from being burnt are important. But more important is not to let the failed risk trap your heart in the cellar of life. Flowers can grow and life can also regenerate and flourish after the fire does its damage. Same with our hearts. A life well lived is a life of continuous growth, change and risk taking, in spite of the burnt experiences you endure. A life well lived is one where we embrace and believe that through nature, God placed the ability to experience Super Bloom not just upon the burnt floor of the forest, but also within us.

Take risk by stepping outside your comfort zone. Take risks by looking at opportunities or situations differently. Taking risk might just lead you down a path that will surprise you about yourself. It might teach you that what you thought impossible is not only possible but incredible. You may learn the limits or rules you put on yourself need adjustment and a re-think.

Super Bloom in a person is achieved by replacing the negative "what-ifs" and fears with exploration and risk taking. Often, what traps us in today's conditions is the memory of being burnt from the past. But memories that limit us need to become ashes that we quit reburning. Fear of risk traps us in what we think is safety and comfort. But what we don't realize is that what we think is safety, is actually a slow death from apathy. It isn't a matter of taking off the blinders, it's a matter of closing your eyes entirely to negative "what-ifs" and fears. It's a matter of dismissing the reasons of why you're saying no. It's a matter of taking a risk by saying yes, exploring, and seeing what happens.

And if one gets burnt again, you will learn, you will grow and in time you will give thanks for the adventure.

Go Super Bloom!

Seeking Clarity

Very few things cleanse the mind like a hike in nature. This week I had the pleasure of spending several days at The Lodge at Falls Creek State Park in Tennessee. Every day, I hiked five to ten miles to see the waterfalls and gorges in this beautiful state park.

On my final day, I decided to go out at dawn for a final hike before departing for Nashville to catch my flight home.

For this morning's trek, I left behind the cell phone and AirPods. It was good to hike through nature without the distractions of music, podcasts, e-mails, texts, and phone calls. Just me, the birds, squirrels, and painted leaves along the lakeside path.

As I hiked, I found myself contemplating how this week of being immersed in fresh air, sun and nature had helped untie the knots and untangle the messes that tend to gather in my brain. As I often do, I also reflected upon how I might improve or do better in my pursuit of living well.

As the morning sun broke through trees in these Cumberland Mountains of Tennessee, memories of a simple message from a simple man jumped to the lead in this mindful journey.

I recalled a moment from my father's 100th birthday when a reporter asked: *"Lloyd — what would you say is the key to a long and happy life?"*

After a few seconds of thought Dad responded with that always present sparkle in his eyes.

He simply said: *"Live each day with love in your heart."*

Clarity hoped for —clarity found.

Airplanes

Today, 150 passengers and six crew. 156 people.

Maybe half headed home, the other half headed out.

Some for work, some for play.

Some going to learn the easy way.

Some must learn the hard way.

A few yearning hearts, a few broken hearts.

Some have been there; some have done that.

Some have so much living yet to be done.

Some old enough to understand much.

Some will live long, and some will die young.

Yes, 150 passengers and six crew,

156 different people.

156 different stories.

The Jagged Edge

Written during a flight over San Francisco on 11/09/01 at 11:30 a.m.

The jagged edges that form the coastline mirror life.

An ocean to the west, the busy metropolis to the east.

The jagged edge stands in transition between the two.

Smooth methodical calming waves.

Clarity, depth, wholeness.

A blue cast of serenity surrenders only to the sun.

Busy business, speeding traffic.

Hard and cold confusion on shallow concrete.

Disorder, clutter. All is a tangle.

An in-between? Again, answers lie in the jagged edge.

Oh, that jagged edge, that transitional jagged edge.

It is the jagged edges of life that bring us to reality.

The transition between the clutter and the serene.

Navigation of the transition brings order and understanding.

Without one, there is no appeal for the other.

Without clutter, there is no serene.

Without serenity, clutter is unknown.

Truth and learning occur in our transitions.

Truth and learning occur upon Jagged Edges.

One Single Light

As I fly home this evening, I am struck first by the enormous vastness of this country and of our world. I can see for miles and miles. Past mountains stretching to touch the nearest cloud. Over farms bursting with crops born of the sweat of man. To rivers that course like veins through the body of our homeland. As I ponder the enormity before me, my attention is drawn to a collection of lights which encompass a city below. Again, I think of the hundreds, no thousands of cities, and villages that sparkle each night as these air vessels circle our globe.

But, as I look to these collections of lights sewn together like a patch to a broken landscape, I begin to focus on one light not the whole, and my mind wonders about that one single light.

Is it a streetlight in a neighborhood where underneath children play, or neighbors talk? Or maybe a night light in a school yard where this morning a little girl was olly olly oxen free or a little boy caught a fly ball. Perhaps this light is at the corner of Walnut and Sharp Streets and stands proud, like a sentry, to offer its security to the stores and pedestrians each and every night of the year.

Perhaps it could be a backyard light of some family not known, where inside sleeps a baby. A baby that someday will grow to be a fireman, or a nurse, and save a life. Or be a teacher, or an electrician or perhaps discover some great cure.

Or perhaps a baby sleeps safely and in peace under my single light. A baby that someday will be flying the heavens as I am now and will also focus and question the role of one single light below. Perhaps that light he now questions brightens the path of this old man who years before focused on his single light. While we may never meet in body, our spirits touched through a time-stretched span, yet only in an unrealized Godly moment. Unrealized by the participants, but connected, and realized by God.

As God brought us unknowingly together, I wonder: did an energy pass between us as we contemplated that one single light? Did I perhaps pass on to that crib some experience or knowledge gathered along my long path that gives him a dream or direction? Years later did he give back to me strength and peace to face my remainder?

The Great Facilitator is the only one who knows and gives a gentle nod to the moment. The moment inspired by one single light below. Without our knowledge or understanding, one single light sometimes lights our way.

One single light created in His gentle and most quiet way.

One Can't Help But Believe

On board American Airlines
Flight 1211. Seat 3A. Omaha to
Dallas. January 17, 1996. 6:58 a.m.

The airplane climbs this early morn from a cold gray airport, winter worn.

Quickly, muted sights of the nighttime lights are blanketed by charcoal clouds.

A dismal day—thoughts say "sleep—just sleep." Maybe another flight will hold sights worthy to keep. In a slight bit of time however, crashing in through my portal comes laser's heat of suddenly warm light upon my face.

When I turn to discover the source of this interruption, my heart jumps at the beauty painted in absolute perfection before me. I feel as though I am flying in the mid layer of some giant, galactic cookie. A thin layer of clarity between two dark ominous blankets.

As I give my attention to the eastern edge, I view the painted middle. A clean, clear blue over a light amber hue. The lower dark layer, covering a city beginning to wake. The upper layer capping the morning sun, begging to be seen. They combine to cause focus on the beauty that lies between.

As the plane gently approaches the upper layer, the clouds seem to be raining down cold and darkness. The underside of this next quest is like the sculptured roof of a cavern, miles below the earth's populated crust.

As we enter this new layer, my portal view turns a gorgeous dark blue with hints of sunlit white splintering through. The amazing deepness of color shadows my disappointment of losing that wondrous view of nature's broken sky.

Suddenly, we break again! Yet another breach of the darkness, full of beauty that reigns. Now as the sun rises in its majestic manner, the amber lights seem to illuminate the lower clouds as though coming from beneath.

The sights ignite my imagination! The visions cast before me cause illusions of ancient times and ancient lands. It's as though a fire is glowing beneath a blanket of powdery snow. Silent beauty explodes around me as mystic colors burst through landscaped clouds.

My transport glides me through this unguided tour of the heaven's great vista. And as it does, I think to myself that no museum holds such treasure. No amusement park offers such an attraction. It was here, before me, for this one moment in time. A gracious beauty too bold to compare, too spacious to contain, and yet too artful to properly explain.

Only my silent thanks I can offer to God above to have been a witness to this most heavenly blessed exhibition. And then, for a moment, I wonder to myself; how could anyone help but believe?

I Am Always With You
An Open Letter to My Loved Ones

When my physical body expires, and I become ashes to the wind and earth, don't grieve for long about your loss, as I will always be with you.

Not just in photos and memories, but I will also be present in your spirit, soul, and heart. I am forever present, and I can hear your silent queries. I will reply to you through your dreams, your intuition, your morals, and your intellect. In all of these, I am present and will share my thoughts with you.

Go forward with confidence that I am forevermore with you.

The 12th Floor

At least once a week I pick my parents up from their Assisted Living complex to take them out to breakfast where we meet up with my kids and grandkids. Their apartment is on the second floor of a very nice Assisted Living complex.

With both parents using walkers, one had better not be in a hurry. I have to remember to use my "extra patience" app that is sometimes, but not always, accessible via my i-brain. As we approach the elevator Dad almost always says to me, "Push the button for the 12th Floor." I gently remind him we are in a two-story building and there is no 12th floor. He gets that well-known twinkle in his eye and says, "Jerry— Heaven is on the 12th Floor and I'm ready to go." We go through the same dialogue upon our return trip almost every time. Today is no different: "Push the button to the 12th Floor."

At 101 years old I guess he has given it a lot of thought. There is no doubt his health is failing. His mind is sharp, but you can see in his body that he is on a rapid decline. In my mind that means that death is probably within a year or so. He is spending more and more time in bed and his activity level is falling. Yet, his mental acuity, orneriness, twinkle, and spry smile remain evident.

Over the next few weeks Dad increases his time in bed to nearly twenty three hours a day for probably five days a week and maybe eighteen hours on the remaining two. He goes from the walker to needing a wheelchair as his legs lose the strength to carry him. But occasionally, whether sitting in his big blue chair or as we approach any elevator he says, "Jerry—push the button to the 12th floor for me."

I typically respond with something along the lines of "Dad—please don't say that." Or "You're not going to the 12th floor today, Dad." Once in a while, he furthers the discussion by telling me he is ready to die, and he doesn't fear it. In retrospect, I think he is doing what he can to prepare me for reality.

One morning, I get a call from the head nurse of assisted living that she feels Dad needs to be evaluated for Hospice. It hits me like a ton of bricks. I think that means they feel death is imminent in days or weeks. I meet the hospice nurse at their apartment later that day and she so sweetly explains to me that it does not mean Dad is close. They will work with him to make him more comfortable and to watch him closely. They will go in six-month increments and they have experienced several people in similar situations graduate and come out of hospice. It is purely an increase in his care and oversight. Intellectually I know Dad is on borrowed time and we have been so blessed to have him with us this long. But just because I know intellectually that he will die sometime soon, it doesn't connect with me emotionally.

A week or two into hospice care Dad gets better and his time in bed runs consistently less and his energy improves. Medically speaking there is nothing wrong with Dad and mentally he is very sharp. His body is simply wearing out.

Still remaining strong is his sense of humor and enjoyment of teasing people, and we all hear more than once—"Take me to the 12th Floor." The nurses ask him—"What's on the 12th floor?" He giggles and has that twinkle and says "Heaven." The nurses tell me often how amazing Dad is and they feel the odds are good he will live for months and maybe make it to his 102nd birthday which is ten months away.

Then suddenly again his energy drops and time in bed increases again back to nearly twenty three hours a day. One day I talk to him on the phone and ask if he wants to go to the family breakfast tomorrow and he says yes. When I get to his apartment that next morning he is in bed, the hospice nurses are with him and all he can do is mumble. He obviously can't go to breakfast, but mom wants to. The nurses tell me that they feel Dad is within weeks, but not days of passing. I take mom to breakfast and upon our return when we walk into the apartment Dad is sitting at the breakfast bar eating a bowl of cereal. He says immediately "Hi Jerry—how is breakfast?" I am so surprised to see him up given his condition when I left less than two hours earlier. We visit for a few minutes and he then says he wants to go back to bed. The nurse and I help him and as I am preparing to leave he says to me—"Jerry make sure you know how to get me to the 12th floor." I say "Dad, don't go there" and kiss him on the cheek goodbye.

The next day the hospice nurses call me and tell me that Dad is progressing towards death. I spend most of the afternoon there with him. He can't talk and appears to be sleeping but comfortable. I leave early that evening and tell them to call me if anything changes otherwise, I will be back the next morning.

The next morning, I arrive at about 8 a.m. and Dad is in the same situation, in bed and pretty much out of it. I stay at his bedside until about 10 a.m.. The nurse on duty tells me he feels Dad is not within hours of death, but maybe within a day or two. I have an early lunch appointment, and the nurse tells me to go to it and if anything changes he will call me.

On the way to my lunch appointment, I call one of my daughters and she says that she and her sister are planning on going to see their grandpa at about 1:00 p.m. I tell them I might meet them there. My lunch appointment ends about 12:30 and as I am walking to my car, I get a phone call from the hospice nurse. He says to me, "You need to get here as soon as possible—your dad is going down faster than we thought." I hurry my travels and while on the way call my daughters. They are already on their way and say they will hurry also.

All three of us arrive at the same time and immediately go to Dad's bedside. He is breathing but appears unconscious. I sneak away for a minute to go into the living room to be with my mom. I tell mom the situation and that the nurse feels Dad will pass away very soon. I ask her if she wants to be in with us and at his side. She says she doesn't want to and that she is fine. She asks me to keep her updated. As I rejoin the kids at Dad's bedside the nurse explains to us that they have signs and items they monitor regarding the death process. Apparently, the skin starts changing in the feet and works its way up the legs. It is what they call "mottling." The nurse tells us that he feels Dad will pass within minutes. I look at the clock and it reads 1:15 pm.

We wait, we talk amongst ourselves, the girls pat Dad's legs and his back as I sit at his bedside and hold his hand. Occasionally I gently rub his forehead and face. About every twenty minutes the nurse checks his pulse and listens to his heart with his stethoscope. Around 3:00 p.m. the nurse states that he doesn't understand why Dad hasn't died. He says he has shown every sign of it for three hours now and it typically doesn't take this long. He says, "I don't get it." Dad isn't struggling and all you can see is a very slight raise and lower of his chest from his shallow breathing.

I then reach up and put my cheek to his cheek and I speak in Dad's ear, while still holding his hand. I say, "Dad this is Jerry. I love you. It's time now for you to push the button to the 12th Floor." I give him a small kiss on his cheek, and I then see a very slight movement in his chin. To me, it is a small nod of understanding. Dad passes away within ten minutes thereafter.

It is one of the most amazing experiences of my life. Now, when visiting buildings with elevators, I see that button for the 12th floor I have a little laugh to myself and wonder if I can stop and pay Dad a visit. Someday I will.

There is no doubt, Dad is on "His" 12th floor. I'm very confident the view is spectacular, and he is there telling stories with that spry smile and twinkle in his eye.

Part Two

Resilience and Growth

This section contains some of my all-time favorites. Many are lectures to myself. In fact, one title I considered for this book was "Talking Out Loud—Mostly to Myself," because so many of these writings were born from trying to straighten out my own head or resolve turbulence within my own mind.

Turbulence is an interesting word for what goes on in our lives and minds daily. Trying to minimize the turbulence is what retirement is all about, I guess. But maybe reducing or managing turbulence is something we should try to do daily, well before retirement. Personally, I think of retirement as reducing the intensity of my work life and increasing the occurrences of family time, pleasurable experiences, and memory building.

I looked up synonyms for turbulence and found: chaos, unrest, confusion, commotion, turmoil. Don't we all have various forms of turbulence in our lives and minds every day?

What does a pilot do when encountering turbulence? They slow to a specific penetration speed, adjust altitude, communicate with air traffic control and other aircraft for smoother air, and deviate course to fly around rough patches. They focus on maintaining control rather than fighting the bumps, using weather radar to proactively avoid the worst of it.

Many of my writings throughout this book—and most specifically in this section—are my own way of dealing with turbulence. Finding smoother air. Communicating. Deviating my course or mind to get through the rough patches and find resilience, or a smoother path.

Maybe a piece or two will help you find smoother air.

That Big Ol' Ball

It dawned on me recently that I have been working my ass off, taking risks, and pushing the proverbial ball up a very steep hill since I was about thirteen years old. That's a long time of pedal to the metal and shoulder to the backside of the ball.

On a couple of occasions that heavy, big ol' ball I was pushing up that steep hill rolled right back over me, smashing me to the ground, tossing me like litter to the gutters. I suffered the pain of the ball's intentions as I lay face down within the gutter, experiencing firsthand the foul taste and odor of failure. But, through the grace of God, the encouragement of family and friends, and an inner belief in myself, I found my drive and rose again, and then once again.

The ups and downs of rising, then falling, getting up only to fail again and again were hurtful, humbling, and educational. Failing then experiencing a rebirth to rise again has taken me to heights I never dreamed possible. Intellectually, spiritually and financially, it seems as though it has all come together now. It's as though an unbelievable and much-appreciated gift has been laid upon my doorstep.

As I now view the tumultuous road that lies behind me and reflect upon my past, I'm filled with gratitude for the lessons, the hill, the ball, the gutter, and the journey along the way.

Friends, associates, and family encouraged my journey through the years. They believed in me, encouraged me, and gave me reason to endure. My heartfelt thanks, love, appreciation and recognition I offer to them as their faces pass through my mind daily.

I'm also grateful for those who threw land mines in my path, opposed my journey or pushed that ball back at me. They hardened my resolve and ignited my competitive nature to not give up or to give in. I'm not going to say they lost, or that I won, as naming a winner doesn't matter at this point. But what means more to me than anything I ever achieved is what I have overcome. Overcoming the land mines, obstacles, and the pushback is my heart and soul's reward. My thanks to those who provided me the opportunity to realize these gifts.

Now the challenge is to learn how to enjoy the rewards I have earned and been blessed with. I need to learn how to stop pushing the ball so hard and so often. I now need to learn how to ride atop that ball and to enjoy the view and the ride. I think there are some potential keys to this new journey of enjoyment.

The first lies in sharing my story with others so that those who are pushing and on their own difficult journey can find some encouragement and lessons of survival. I also think great enjoyment will come my way as I share the rewards I have been blessed with among those less fortunate, those I care about and with those I love. Finally, I think it is time to get some enjoyment out of those rewards myself personally without feeling guilty about it, or wasteful. This latter mission is the hardest. I have not found it easy to enjoy my own rewards as they are often followed by feelings of wastefulness, guilt, or unworthiness. This is where I have the most work to do.

Figuring out how to pursue these three missions in balance and in earnest will be my challenge. Yet I don't want to give up quite yet on pushing that big ol' ball either. It has brought me a lot of joy, rewards, and has served me well. Unlike the first half of the journey, I now know how to control that ball so that it will never roll back over me again. Stay in control of the ball, own the ball, ride the ball, and keep it rolling forward as I learn how to have balance in sharing, giving and enjoying.

The Demon of Death

Live as though the demon of death rides upon your shoulder every day.

At any time, it can jump in your path and steal you away.

With this passenger aboard, you have choices before you; which do you take?

Do you cower and sit to gather dust while you await the demon's lust?

Or do you attack your goals to extract every ounce from the bones of life?

Choose to wait and you energize that demon of death each and every day.

Choose to live and to attack life, and that waiting assassin keeps to the back.

The demon has no say.

'Tis yours to decide each and every day.

Fertile Ground

I have a problem. Okay, maybe more than one problem—I have problems!

I have been exploring and investigating the source of these problems and today I came to a stark realization.

I'm my problem.

My friends (past or present) are not the source of my problems. My employer or associates are not the source either.

My family really isn't to blame. Nor are my problems the result of past relationships. In truth, I can't blame that photo from the past.

It's hard to admit, but it's true!

How I was raised isn't the cause of my problem either. And neither are the obstacles or traumas I have faced responsible for the troubles that seem to plague me now.

Somehow, I mentally awoke today and finally accepted that the dilemmas I have are traced singularly to that space that lies between my ears. Yep, in that brain of mine.

Problems that live in this space are instigated by me and nurtured by me. I allow them to take seed and I even water and fertilize them from time to time.

Acceptance that there is no one to blame, no past to blame and only me to blame, helps me cleanse the stale blame.

Sure, I have issues to resolve and problems to cure or fix. Yet to cast blame for these has been nothing but an endless ticket to keep riding that carousel, round and round we go!

From this day forward, I shall take sole responsibility for my problems and no longer cast blame to others or conditions past or present.

I will accept that I and I alone am the source of what I view as problems. From now on, I will take responsibility to help release these toxic views and haunting thoughts.

This way, I can make room for new problems and other issues to take seed in that fertile ground that lies between my ears.

Shhhhh—No Is Speaking

Shhhhh—No is Speaking.

Finding Yes is like the blind traversing the maze.

You bounce off the Nos.

You turn, you try another way.

No is not an end.

No is but a detour to Yes.

You will hear a lot of No.

No needs to be your fuel.

Always remember, No is Yes—just not now.

If you listen closely No will give you direction to Yes.

Listen closely to the why in the No.

Listen for the quiet directions to Yes.

They are there, deep inside the No.

"Shhhhh—No is Speaking."

Fire in the Belly!

I was asked today, how to succeed?
A burning desire so many wish to seed.
I've seen plenty with hunger to achieve.
And dreams and prayers of what to be.

They want of glory and freedom to play.
But are they willing, with sacrifices to pay?

For most I have known that have achieved,
were not smarter or luckier or given to succeed.
Most if not all paid a great price for their glory.
Most, if not all, had blood, sweat and tears in their story.

. . .

They work while others are at home to rest.

Each day they put themselves to new tests.

They accept risk and challenge without hesitation

and study and work beyond others' expectations.

They know the ultimate reward lies not in a check,

but in the satisfaction and fulfillment of self-respect.

So when you say you want high stakes.

I ask are you willing to do what it takes?

Is the fire in your belly strong enough to sustain

when the critics and setbacks come like rain?

Is your will and dedication committed to stay?

Are you willing to work while others play?

Can you stomach risk and fight the sharks?

Can you face failure then once again start?

For when you say you want a big slice

I look to your heart and ask, "Will you pay the price?"

History's Heroes

Reading about great people of the past provides us a compass to deal with the future in a manner in which we can take pride in our decisions.

When I read of the sacrifices of George Washington, Meriwether Lewis or Martin Luther King, I learn of the persistence and patience required of the long struggle.

When I read of Thomas Jefferson, James Madison, and Malcolm X, I learn of the importance of freedom, individual human rights, and self-esteem.

When I read of General Marshall or Abraham Lincoln, I learn about leadership, conciliation, and forgiveness.

The words and examples of Winston Churchill and Ronald Reagan teach me about democracy and citizenship.

There is more to their stories than important historical events. The value of each lies within their character and dedication at all costs to their convictions. They exemplify *"to thy own self be true."*

This is why we must study the past—to enrich our moral character with true life examples, give us mental battery to stay the course, and to grow confidence in pursuit of our own moralities and beliefs.

50

Shoes and Dreams

Unlike shoes, dreams aren't supposed to fit you today.

Nope. Dreams are supposed to be much bigger than you are.

You buy shoes that fit you today, but you want dreams you have to grow into.

Doors

Such simple, ordinary, utilitarian things. Yet they can be a metaphor for living. Doors bring transition. Some are new, some are old, some are big, some are small, some are bright, some are dingy.

Doors come in many colors. Some are glass, some are iron, some are open, some are closed. But whatever they are or are not, it is what they represent, protect, or offer, that is important.

What do the doors in your life bring to you?

... open and meet happiness.

... close to forget.

... walk through for opportunity.

... ignore and miss out.

... lock for security.

... open to risk.

... slam in anger.

... knock for permission.

... look through in hope.

... break down to achieve.

... past to future.

... respect doors.

... love doors.

... understand doors.

... recognize doors.

... they are life.

... they are living.

They are Doors.

Life, What It Isn't and What It Is All About

Life isn't about keeping score.

It's not about how many friends you either have or don't have.

Or how accepted or admired you are by others.

It's not about if you have plans this weekend or if you're alone.

It isn't about who you're dating, who you used to date, how many people you've dated, or if you haven't been with anyone at all.

It isn't about who has a crush on you or who you have a crush on.

It isn't about who your family is or how rich they are.

It's not about what kind of car you drive. Or where you went to school.

It's not about how good-looking you are or aren't.

It's certainly not about how athletic or strong you are.

Or what clothes you wear, or what kind of music you listen to.

It's not about whether your hair is blonde, red, black, brown or gone.

Or if your skin is too light or too dark, or what color or shade it is.

No, life isn't about what grades you get or how smart you are or aren't.

It's not about what clubs you belong to or how good you are at this sport or in this or that profession.

It isn't about how many trophies you've won or how many times you finished on top.

Life isn't about physical possessions, where you have been or what you have done.

Life just isn't.

But life is about who you show charity to and who you hurt.

It's about whether you purposely help or purposely harm others.

It's about being trustworthy and honoring one's trust in you.

It's about family, friendship, and loyalty to those close to you.

It's about using your words carefully to help and not hurt others.

It's about not spreading gossip and rumors.

It's about what judgments you pass and why.

It's about suppressing jealousy, fear, ignorance, and revenge.

It's about promoting love and erasing inequalities.

It's about having a curiosity about the world and the people around you.

It's about caring for people, all people.

It's about having goals and dreams and a sense of urgency about their pursuit.

It's about growing your knowledge and keeping your brain and spirit alive and vibrant.

But most of all, it's about using your life to touch other people's hearts in such a way that will have a positive impact on them.

You choose the way you live your life, and those choices are what life's all about.

Balance, My Friend, Balance

When we are young, we must learn the advantages of patience and gain understanding that the charging bull many times only feels the sting of the lance to the cheers of the crowd.

However, as we grow older, we must beware not to mistake patience for complacency nor to replace a sense of urgency with an overabundance of study.

Balance, my friend, balance.

I Breathe In, I Breathe Out

I breathe in, I breathe out.

The mind I try to cleanse with every breath.

The mind, I try to relax with every breath.

I breathe slowly in. I breathe out.

I am told not to think, but to get lost in the breath.

I stay quiet and try to do as instructed.

I breathe in and I breathe out.

But I am not lost. My mind is in search.

Search to solve the wants,

Search to resolve the needs.

I breathe in, I breathe out.

I feel my breath, I hear my breath.

I feel my wants, I feel my needs.

I hear my wants; I hear my needs.

I breathe in, I breathe out.

Wishes and needs, please leave me alone.

Please leave me alone while I breathe.

Leave this mind, leave this heart.

Go to my toes, go to my elbows, just let go of my mind.

Let me breathe in, let me breathe out,

Let me breathe in quiet peace.

Please, just for a few minutes today, leave me alone.

To breathe in, to breathe out.

All I Can Do

Every day I have something I need to do or want to do. Every day, doing **All I Can Do**, drives me or energizes me. I know or feel it is never enough. And I'm sure there is more I could tack on. Perhaps my biggest perplexity in life is in figuring out which priority should win today's "**All I Can Do**."

Every morning, during a cup of coffee or two and typically while driving to my office, or maybe while sitting in my favorite chair, I think of the people I love. I think of their lives and our interactions. I think about what is going on with them and wonder if there is anything I can do to help them or enhance their life. Their happiness is of my utmost importance. Whatever I achieve in business or financially means nothing to me without them in my life. The quality of our interactions and time together greatly depends upon their well-being, their fulfillment. The quality of my life is directly affected by the quality of their lives. I always want and try to do **All I Can Do** to love them and help them.

Almost every day there may be appointments or meetings to attend or there may be a load of emails or phone calls that await my reply.

Making progress on business interests seems to always be on my mind. Whether it be to create new opportunities or to protect existing interests, each day I do **All I Can Do** to make good business decisions and to take action to make progress. Every day, I do **All I Can Do**.

There are things that need my attention to keep my surroundings from falling to disarray. The house needs work, the yard needs attention, the clutter needs to be decluttered. I try the best I can to do **All I Can Do**. The car needs to be fixed, the office has issues. I have to try to do **All I Can Do** to address them.

But sometimes I lose sight of what I need to do in order to do a great job of doing **All I Can Do**. Sometimes I forget or put to the back of the line, taking care of me. On this objective, I often fail to do **All I Can Do**.

I need to change this priority in order to do a better and long-lasting job of doing **All I Can Do** for my priorities. I need to find better balance. I need to breathe, relax and breathe. I need to take better care of the vessel that carries my soul, heart and source of energy into the future.

That would be the least I could do to be able to do **All I Can Do**.

Understand Me

I am motivated by the challenge born of the problem.

I am inspired by the height of the obstacle that lies in front of me.

Fear is my ally, urgency is my creed.

Risk moves me to action, 'tis security I loathe.

The hunt always exceeds the feast.

I live and search for the challenge, the risk, the hunt.

When the challenge ends and boredom sets in.

Another venue shall call me out to the cold of the night.

The risk of the unknown shall guide me once again

to the warmth of uncharted waters.

Part Three

Family

"Happiness comes of the capacity to feel deeply, to enjoy simply, to think freely, to risk life, to be needed."

— *Storm Jameson*

When I first saw that quote, it spoke to my heart about family. My happiness comes from deep love for my daughters and grandkids, and the simple times we share together. I heard someone say once that their children were their oxygen—I understand that completely. My kids and grandkids are as essential to my life as breathing.

But family also brings worry, anguish, and pain. It's been said that a parent can never be any happier than their most unhappy child. When we witness their struggles, we live it too. We want to fix everything and take away their hurt, but we can't and shouldn't. Allowing them to work through their challenges gives them the same education we experienced.

One element that shapes these writings is the absence of family in my own childhood. My mother's parents died before she was sixteen. My father's parents moved to Florida when I was born, and I barely knew them. My brother, seven years older, died at twenty-eight—we'd had a distant, difficult relationship. So I grew up without the guidance of grandparents and without a close sibling bond.

Having kids and grandkids filled a hole I didn't even know was there. Today, my cup runneth over with the love and value they bring to my life. I hope that comes through in these writings.

First One ~ Then Two!

F irst one baby, then two.

One starts school, then two.

One needs a leotard, then somehow two.

One wants a car, and soon follows: you need one too?

Prom dress one, Prom dress two.

I may be getting the hang of this "one then two."

First off to college, right behind comes number two.

Wedding dress number one. Then wedding dress number two.

What's this? A grandbaby on my lap!

I get it! Sometime soon!

First comes one, then comes two!

WHAT A MESS!!!

I t's early Sunday morning and light is beginning to break through the paned windows of my living room.

I'm sitting in the corner and casting my eyes about the room and my first thoughts are *"What a mess."*

My right hand holds my favorite weekend coffee cup. A heavy white porcelain diner-type cup.

The cup reminds me of Mom.

The coffee is good and hot, the scent whispers to me "It's time to get up and start breakfast."

Different this morning from my typical Sunday morning, however, is that it appears a tornado hit this room last night without so much as a warning siren or a weather bulletin.

Seeing a jumbled mess here is unusual. At least unusual for me and especially this room.

To have disarray typically means that I didn't fold last night's blanket or I forgot to put the remote in its proper holder or even worse, I left a wine glass with its red-stained reminder on the coffee table.

But this morning, there isn't just one blanket unfurled in the room but three or four. Everything is out of place.

Books are scattered, games are half-played, juice boxes and straw wrappers adorn my coffee table and floor.

And yet, I smile. I should get up and start breakfast or maybe pick up, but I'm enjoying the scene of the crime, the havoc's aftermath, the storm's result.

Anyway, if I got up and walked to the kitchen, I might very well trip over the stuffed animals or, more likely trip over the smile on my heart.

Then suddenly, one of the blankets on the couch starts to move much like a small wave. I sip some coffee and I wait. Yes, I'm certain I saw a slight movement come from within that cocoon.

My smile grows as I'm anxious to see which animal might be ready to rise. Happiness and gratitude fill me as I recall the giggles and fun from last night.

My favorite cup rises to deliver again. Breakfast can wait. Picking up or cleaning this mess can wait. I then realize: I need this mess. This mess is good for me. I love this mess; yes—I truly love having this mess.

The blanket moves again and a small head starts to peek out. Eyes are blinking to adjust to the light of day. Then suddenly she spots me staring at her from the corner of the room. She gets that spry little smile on that beautiful face shining out from her mop of tangled hair and she says with her craggy morning voice: "Hi Grandpa!"

Mess? What mess?

One Remarkable Tree

When nothing makes sense, or the world seems upside down.

Then go to your special tree for a warm-hearted place to lean.

If someone you care about turns on you or hurts you.

One comforting tree will be there that you can lean into.

Should you have a difficult decision to make and need an ear.

That one unique tree will be there to listen and care.

That reliable tree is also a great place to share.

Your successes, your love story, your dreams from here to there.

Since the day you were born to the day you die.

One remarkable tree stands ready and by your side.

Learn to lean on your tree any time you feel the need.

Come to us, and lean on your strong and forever-loving,

Family Tree

A Message From Your Child

Is there a heaven, or is there a hell?

Perhaps there are only memories of you, that I shall someday tell.

Decisions you make create stories that within my memory forever dwells.

Maybe this is your spirit, your legacy, your heaven, or your hell.

Will your story be positive examples full of love and positive giving?

Or will it be of anger, hurt and negative living?

Will your spirit sustain for generations a story to tell?

Or will your energy fade fast away where it first fell?

This is a story that only you shall make.

A story that only you can create.

'Tis up to you to determine, is it your heaven or shall it be your hell?

Either way know this, it's your decision, but a story that I shall live to tell.

Conflict and Comfort on College Day

Leaving her there wasn't as hard to do as I thought it would be. Not that it was easy. My heart was in my throat and yes, my face felt the wetness of my sorrow.

But still, I felt a certain confidence. Confidence I had not anticipated, but should have. Knowing that she could handle this new adventure comforted me.

While she and I react differently to challenges, she always achieves victory.

I know her conservative nature and dedication to her goals will keep her safe.

Her focus is enviable, and my faith in her is without question.

The sadness burdening my heart comes from selfishly missing her company.

Conflicts between my heart and logic, between my selfishness and her growth are enormous. But I know which must and shall prevail. And in this, I shall also grow.

For as she has often quoted, "That which does not kill you makes you stronger." And strength within me must also follow.

Her physical presence can never be replaced.

But her spirit, strong within my heart, will offer comfort along the way.

As departure came near, I reviewed my mental checklist: The dorm room is ready and supplies within reach.

The books have been purchased and the ATM card is ready in case of need.

Registration is done and her fall schedule complete.

One more thing before I go that I almost forgot. A lecture from Dad...

Forget it, there is no need.

Thoughts from the Parent of a Gymnast

Her hands bleed from the grip of the bar.

My little girl wants to be a star.

Ice upon the knees and ankles,

A price to pay for all the medals.

Controlled contortions in the air.

My gymnast flies where others don't dare.

I wonder at times have I done right?

The pain, the tears, the risk of flight.

But then I consider the reward versus risk.

Beyond the medals, the fun, the travels we list.

With the confidence she has gained.

Her life will never be restrained.

Her focus, her drive, her dedication.

Values not taught through education.

God, I only pray for you to spot her clear.

Should you foresee a tragic fall come near.

For the sport that brings her so much.

I would pray not take away her loving touch.

My beautiful girl hugs me after the meet.

One more meet's routines, now safely complete.

She is the Daughter, and I am the Dad

Reflections From the Father of a 13-Year-Old Girl

She is the daughter. She works hard to learn the lessons offered by education, activities, and life.

I am the Dad. I work hard to do what is right. To lead, to counsel, to provide, and *to drive and to pay.*

She is the daughter. Her rewards are growth, experience, recognition, confidence, intelligence, and fulfillment.

I am the Dad. My rewards are her smile, her growth, her hugs, her respect, and four simple words: *"I love you, Dad."*

Yes, she is the daughter, and I am the Dad.

Daddy Take a Look at Me

In her words, "Daddy did you see?" is a message God's sending to me.

The words of this precious little girl come straight from heaven above.

Saying: "Hey Daddy I'm growing up, stop and take a look at me."

Don't listen to the words but hear the message clear.

It won't be long, she'll be grown and gone, and you'll long for her.

Daddy do you see My Little Pony has a brand-new doo?

Daddy did you see me? A great hand stand I can do.

Oh Daddy come and see a new dance I'll do for you.

Daddy did you see? Daddy did you hear? Daddy stop and take a look at me.

Dad will you be at my recital? Are you coming to the game tonight?

Sometimes I feel the pressures on to work my life away.

But all I have to do is remember that message that's in plain sight.

Daddy did you try the new recipe I made for you?

Daddy did you see the back flip I can do?

Oh Daddy come and see, a new cheer we're about to do.

Daddy did you see? Daddy did you hear? Daddy stop and take a look at me.

Yo Dad—did you see the great movie the other night?

Hey Dad, do you like the college I'm checking out?

My little girl is now a lady and there is a message she's sending tonight.

The message is in plain sight, if only I stop to see it right.

It won't be long, she'll be grown and gone far, far out of sight.

Daddy did you like the dress I wore for you?

Daddy will you be there when I say I do?

Oh Daddy come and see, a new grandson we have for you!

Daddy did you see? Daddy did you hear? Daddy stop and take a look at me!

Yes, the message is clear and there for all to see; Daddy, come and take a look at me.

More Not Less

My mother is ninety and my father is ninety-six. I am witnessing firsthand the effects that aging has on us all. Not just them or me, but everyone around us.

As I reflect on the changes—in personalities, needs, reactions, feelings, and all the interactions that come with this process—the word "more" keeps rolling around in my mind. More for them, more from me, more from all of our family. More of this, more of that. A lot more of the more and yet I know more is yet to come.

More. That word crashes and slams around my mind in a vast array of combinations.

While today I may seem overwhelmed by more, I know that someday, more will turn not to less, but to mere memories and wishes for more.

The "More" of aging:

More history than future.

More love than hassle.

More slow than go.

More advice than correction.

More yesterdays than tomorrows.

More acceptance than denial.

More history than future.

More forget than regret.

More fragile than agile.

More give than take.

More memories than dreams.

More need than want.

More meds than ever.

More doctors than friends.

More time not less...

Please, please, I'm begging for _more time_, not less.

A Man I Call Dad

His body grows tired now. I can hear it in his voice and see it in his step.

It has taken me too long to appreciate this gentle man I call Dad.

It was always there for me to see, but my race along life's highway got in my way.

From childhood to adulthood, his example always was there.

His gentle heart guided his gentle hand and most gentle way.

Seeing the best in us all, he always put our family first.

He never carries a grudge or attempts to be our judge.

He just loves us, helps us, and shows he's proud of us.

He gives far more than he takes, this gentle man I call Dad.

Other people know him first and foremost as their friend.

They love him for the twinkle in his eyes, his energy, his laugh.

To many he's a builder of homes. But more so to me, a builder by example.

An example of hard work, an example of gentle ways, a builder of family.

An honest man, a simple man, a family man.

A gentle man with a gentle heart and gentle hand.

A man I call my Dad.

To this day his energy yet amazes all.

That twinkle, that smile to all they still show full.

Yet, I hear in his voice and I see in his step that his body grows old.

I know not when the candle shall give way.

But when this gentle man shall see that final day

I'll take solace as memories and examples never fade away.

Memories of his gentle heart, his gentle hand and his most gentle way.

I'm so blessed to get to say; he is the man that I call Dad.

Lloyd Banks on his 100th birthday. April 25, 1921 – June 1, 2022 (101 years old)

No One Told Him

He wants to be on the go. He wants to see family and friends. His mind can't stop even though his body can't keep up. I guess no one told him he wasn't supposed to live this long.

He wants to build houses, mow yards and go places. His mind can't stop, even though his body can't keep up. I guess no one told him he wasn't supposed to live this long.

He bought long-term care insurance almost 40 years ago, which he still makes payment on, just in case. While his mind can't stop, his body just can't keep up. I guess no one told him he wasn't supposed to live this long.

He visits his parents and old friends in stories and memories that are clean and clear as the sun. Seems as though his mind can't stop even though his body can't keep up. I guess no one told him he wasn't supposed to live this long.

Nope, he wasn't supposed to live this long. And I'm filled with gratitude that no one ever told him.

What it Means
to be a Parent

It means loving them, caring for them, nurturing them, forgiving them, leading them, teaching them, listening to them and setting an example for them of what it is to be a good human being.

It means allowing them to fail. Allowing them to venture out. Expecting them to find their own path. Allowing them to make mistakes and to figure out solutions. Expecting them to do their best.

It means not getting in the way of their education. You learned from your mistakes, failures, and setbacks. Now allow them the same opportunity.

It means putting guardrails and boundaries on your protection of them, especially as they grow up.

It means being a role model and teacher of responsibility, hard work, ethics, honesty, dreaming, determination, discipline and resiliency.

It means making sacrifices in your own wants, dreams and life to be present for them and to provide for them.

Primarily it means loving them, but not just in words—but in actions.

<u>What being a parent doesn't mean.</u>

It doesn't mean you need to be their best friend. You aren't a contemporary of theirs, you're an adult role model.

You don't need to dress like them, use their linguistics, or be into whatever they are into. Understand those elements and be aware, yes. Use them yourself or try to be just like them, no.

It doesn't mean you are always trying to gain their approval or trying to make them happy. Life isn't always fair and it isn't always happy.

Help them learn how to deal with adversity and to learn resiliency.

Traveling Home

I grew up in a small town surrounded by farms located in the beautiful hills of southwest Iowa and have always lived nearby. But that hasn't limited my life experiences.

I have seen and done much as I have traveled the globe and experienced life to the fullest extent I reasonably could.

I have seen the ravages of war upon a country and its people from the streets of Saigon.

I experienced the breach of the bus-sized whale off the coast of Hawaii and a day later helicoptered over the volcanic eruption of Kilauea.

Big Ben chimed for all to hear as we passed over the Thames River. The next day I sat in the bunker from which decades prior, Churchill managed the troops to victory while Hitler's bombs of terror shattered buildings and lives above.

One afternoon, I saw the sunshine through the stained-glass dormers of the Vatican then later walked the famed streets of Rome where Marcus Aurelius once rode victoriously upon his chariot.

I gazed at Michelangelo's "David" in Florence one morning then that evening drank wine at a street side café in a walled village of Tuscany.

I've snacked upon grapes and cheese floating on a small vessel in the bay of Cinque Terre while the youthful captain spoke of the legends and history of his homeland.

Side by side I stood with my daughters 984 feet above the ground as we viewed the lights of Paris from a tower built by Gustave Eiffel in the late 1800s.

My grandson and I drove the backroads of Spain and were moved by the architecture of Gehry in Bilbao, the audacity of Gaudí in Barcelona, and the whimsy of Salvador Dalí in Cadaqués.

I once stood in the Salzburg home where Mozart was born and a few days later attended a classical concert in Vienna, the City of Music.

I was blessed to walk the streets and visit the buildings in Warsaw that communism once destroyed but the strength of survivors and prayers of freedom rebuilt.

After listening to a Shaman speak his truth at the Mayan ruins of Tulum, I went diving among the coral reefs of the Caribbean and later sat with my feet in the sand while eating lobster on the beaches of Mexico.

I have walked the halls of Monticello where the author of *The Declaration of Independence* lived while his slaves worked in the cellars below not able to live his words of freedom.

All in one day, I visited two sites famous to the world for occurrences a century apart but linked together by human color. In the morning, I sat at the desk where Abraham Lincoln signed the Emancipation

Proclamation and later that day stood where Mahalia Jackson encouraged Martin Luther King Jr. to tell the world about his dream.

I have grieved at the site where over 3,000 people died from terrorism yet later that year rode snowmobiles among the buffalo in Yellowstone.

I have driven the coastal highway in California and viewed Seattle from atop a needle.

I love to travel and have been blessed to see the world and have more yet to explore.

Yet of all the places I have journeyed there exists one special place that rises above the rest.

I call it home. Home is where my heart finds its peace. Home is not about a city, or a state. It isn't about a favorite team or the best restaurant or an incredible view.

Home is wherever my family and friends reside as their love triumphs over history, scenery, or significance.

Home is where I make a conscious choice to be.

Home is where I always long to be.

Home is where I'm meant to be.

Very Important Things

I do important things. Very important things.

Many people would give anything to do these important things. To me, these are life and death important things.

These important things I do, they inspire me every day.

Very important things they certainly are. Very important.

Spending time with my family is this very important thing I do.

You Can't Reburn
Old Ashes

Dad died June 1, 2022. He was 101 and up until the end his mind was overall pretty good for someone of his age. Dad was always a good talker and loved to tell stories especially about his days on the railroad. But give Dad about any subject and he could find a relatable story to tell.

Mom, on the other hand, was a listener. She didn't talk much and when Dad was present she could hardly get a word in. As they grew old, Mom's patience for Dad's stories waned. More than once she would interrupt the start of one of his stories and announce "Lloyd, we have heard it before." It typically didn't do any good as he would reply with something like "Well, they need to hear it again."

Mom was a young 94 at the time of Dad's death. Still able to think and talk and make decisions. She transitioned to a walker and later a wheelchair, but like Dad, her mind was relatively sharp for a person of her age.

For years our family gathered almost every Sunday at a diner in South Omaha called Louie M's Burger Lust. It is an iconic restaurant with wood floors, brick walls, tin ceilings and loads of memorabilia on the wall. But what made Burger Lust special beyond explanation was their staff and their food. Over the years they knew us and we knew them. We were on a first-name basis and they knew what each person liked to drink or eat. Add to this their iconic food such as a breakfast burrito or their spinach-feta omelet. Every person had a favorite.

A typical gathering would include Mom and Dad, myself, my two daughters, two sons-in-law and seven grandkids. If you have a calculator that should add up to fourteen. We almost always had the big round table at the back with a couple of four-tops added on. On occasion someone would be missing due to sports, or illness but every Sunday for years, whoever was able, knew Sunday breakfast, 9:30am, Burger Lust. Be there or be square!

The first Sunday after Dad's death we met there again and left a chair open to commemorate and remember Dad. It was a tough first Sunday but a nice tradition to continue on. We all committed that our Burger Lust tradition would last as long as Mom was alive. She lived east of Burger Lust about ten miles and the rest of us live to the West about fifteen miles or so.

To get Mom to Burger Lust I would leave my home early and travel twenty five miles to the east to pick Mom up and to be able to transport her safely back to the west about ten miles to Burger Lust. After breakfast I had to retrace my trek to return her to her Assisted Living apartment. Once she was in a wheelchair it was quite an ordeal but well worth it as we got to see her interact with her great-grandkids.

On one very memorable trek from her apartment to Burger Lust she says to me quite matter-of-factly, "Well—your dad was in the room last night." While quite surprised I replied to her "Well, Mom, I'm sure Dad misses you." In my mind, I'm thinking to myself is this dementia, the result of a dream, or did Dad's spirit really visit her. I will just play along and see where this goes.

She then tells me "Yeah, he wouldn't shut up and just kept talking." I told her again, "Mom, I'm sure he misses you." She continued, "With him talking so much, I can't get any sleep." I didn't know what to say but I'm now becoming a believer as it sounds like Dad!

We are now a good ten minutes into our drive with about five miles left when she asks me "Didn't you have him cremated?" I replied, "Yes, Mom—we talked about this, and that is what you and he said you wanted done." She continues, "I know, but you would have thought that would have taken care of that problem." I was surprised and said, "What problem?" She says, "Him visiting and talking so much."

I then try to explain to my dear mother that it is probably his spirit visiting her and the cremation was just his physical body and not his spirit. "Again, Mom, I'm sure Dad misses you and was just visiting and had a lot to tell." She sits with a somewhat disgusted look on her face while I park the car.

After breakfast we get Mom loaded back up and I head back east towards her apartment. After a few minutes, here we go again! She says to me, "So you had Dad cremated?" "Yes, Mom, I did, just like we talked." She then says, "Where are the ashes?" I replied, "They are at my house, Mom." She sits and thinks for a minute and then says, "Well, do you think we should have it done again? It sure didn't seem to work the first time."

Mom, you can't reburn ashes!

Part Four

Reflections on Living Well and Ongoing Questions

It occurs to me that my writing often expresses various shades of gray on whatever happens to be on my mind. My writing comes alive when the right side of my brain is allowed to take over. In my day-job world of real estate investments, the artistic side stays in the background while the left side rules my Excel spreadsheets. I have questioned at times whether my writing in shades of gray is genetically influenced—my mother's maiden name was Evelyn Gray, and she used it in naming me Jerry Gray Banks—or simply a matter of wanting an escape from the black-and-white world of investments. Another question for future exploration.

There are always questions in life, some of which have no concrete answers. I like to take a topic and dig into the harder questions. In "Hate the Hate," I explore that heavy subject in a lighthearted but serious way. "I Am Who I Am" grew out of my dating history. "Simple" started as whimsical but turned serious—written during the COVID pandemic, its positions are perhaps even more relevant today. And when I tackled "Life: What It Isn't and What It Is About," it began as a letter to my grandson but became a letter to myself—a reminder of what matters and, perhaps more significantly, what doesn't. It remains one of my favorites.

Of course, there are certain queries that demand an absolute black-and-white answer, such as: Do you like coconut? *No.* There's zero shades of gray on that topic for me! Eating coconut is like eating a wax candle in my opinion. But in areas such as attitude, love, acceptance, rejection, and politics, these are matters of perspective. I don't pretend to have all the answers. What I offer is some prodding and poking.

Hopefully, these writings will help you find your own answers to topics that seem to live in shades of gray. As it always has been, there always will be ongoing questions.

Rearview Mirrors and Windshields

Tough endings can lead one to new beginnings if you have your mind and heart looking in the right direction.

Tough endings deserve reflection about the why, the how, the process.

What could one have done differently?

Was the end the right or the wrong choice?

When over, the rearview mirror serves a purpose.

But focusing on the mirror too long and missing the view the front windshield offers can lead to a wreck.

At some point you have to take your eyes and mind off the mirror.

At some point one has to start looking and trusting the view to the front.

Once you make the transition from the mirror to the windshield, tough endings will turn into new beginnings.

I Know Who I Am and I Know Who I Am Not

I'm not your six pack abs man.

I'm not your big ol' muscle man.

I'm not your tall, dark, and handsome man.

Nope, not me, not now, never will be.

I'm the workin' man, the come-home man.

I'm the tell-the-truth man, the be-there man.

I'm the love my family, love my country man.

Yep, that's me, now and tomorrow that's who I'll be.

I'm not your bad boy or your partyin' man.

I'm not your fightin' man, or your gamblin' man.

I'm not your pretty boy man, or your singin' man.

Nope, not me, not now, never will be.

I'm your honest man, your get-it-done man.

I'm just your funny man, your lovin' man.

I'm only a plain man, your average Joe man.

Yep, that's me, now and tomorrow that's who I'll be.

Can you live without who I'm not?

Can you live with who I am?

'Cause I know who I'm not and never will be.

Cause I know who I am and always will be.

Please take me as I am or leave me now for who I'm not!

For I'm not those other ways and never will be.

For I am who I am and always will be.

My Style

I'm just being me when I'm in my worn and holy blue jeans, an old t-shirt, and a sweat-soaked farm cap.

They fit the mindset of me—a guy who really doesn't give a crap.

My suburban-living daughters think the jeans should be immediately tossed out.

What they don't know is on a hot day, these jeans vent the places I care most about.

My shirt is just starting to feel right. The neck and sleeves are worn out at the hem.

The holes might be from battery acid or perhaps were snagged on a barbed wire fence.

Some think my hat reeks like sweaty socks and looks like I'm on my last dime.

But just like an old friend, it's gonna be with me for a long, long time.

Yeah, I might stink a bit in my favorite duds. I'm told they're a trashy sight.

If you think I look like I don't care, I have to agree—you'd be seriously right.

When I'm wearing what I want, I'm happy not being a stylish man.

I honestly don't give a shit. And happy to say, that's just who I am.

If the scent of my hat or look of my labor-worn duds say I'm below your class.

Then maybe, just maybe, you're the one who is the egotistical dumbass.

Believe!

Inside the tangles and barbs of rust attempting to confine you to the past, there exists a glimmer of light that craves to lead you to new experiences, peaceful existence, and boundless fulfillment.

Live with gratitude for the light within you!

Believe in your potential!

Believe in your dreams!

Believe in yourself!

Believe in the light within!

Just simply believe!

"A glimmer of light inside the tangles and barbs" – by Jerry Banks.

Simple

When I call for a simple answer, I hear *"Push one for this, push two for that and three, four, five, six or seven for who knows what."*

When all I want is a simple cup of black coffee, I'm asked *"Latte, Cappuccino or Frappuccino? Dark or Light? Tall, Grande or Venti? Hot or iced?"*

When I introduce myself, there are questions to be considered. Is this with a handshake, an elbow touch, a fist bump, or God forbid a hug?

Are we limited to six feet apart or is there some chance I can give or get a simple smile without covering the mug?

Today there's even a complicated tension that holds back a simple conversation between old friends.

Will we discuss politics or events of the day, or do we avoid it like it will poison our friendship?

I wish and want for simple again. Simple times, simple answers, simple lives, simple acceptance, simple living.

Simple faith in the goodness of others.

Simple tolerance of differences or beliefs.

I want to make this very plain and simple.

I only want for simple.

A Little and a Lot!

When we reach that point where we need someone to wipe the Jell-O from our chin or look to others to simply exist day to day.

There will be very little that means a lot and a lot that will mean very little.

A lot of house, a lot of money, a lot of this, or a lot of that will mean very little.

But those little relationships, those little memories, those little loved ones.

Those are the little things that will mean a whole lot.

Life's Reversals

Sour is only sour because there is sweet.

A lie is not a lie without the truth.

Turmoil is only realized as turmoil after observing calm.

We must experience sadness to understand happiness.

One must traverse through thorns to appreciate the path.

Setbacks often guide us forward.

Have gratitude for your setbacks.

Go Conquer Your Maze!

When I enter the maze, I move forward, hit walls, and change direction. Sooner or later, I conquer that damn thing!

Managing one's life is much like trying to solve the maze. If one lives, one can't help but hit walls. You then change direction; you move on. Sooner or later, you will conquer your issue.

Engage the challenge of the labyrinth with spirit. Go forward, hit walls, change direction, and move on.

Go conquer your maze!

It's all part of that most magnificent and beautiful tangled, jumbled, and muddled experience that we call living.

Are We Blind?

Some people are blind, and all they can sense is what they hear or physically feel.

Others are colorblind and see the world in shades of gray.

But what if we were all blind to people's faces and bodies, and all we could see was their soul?

Would we see volumes of love and kindness that lie within them?

Could we measure their intent of help versus harm?

Or might we see hatred and negativity that rule their world?

Would we judge them differently than we otherwise do?

Would we incarcerate those whose souls are good but who made a mistake?

Would we let those who are filled with hate yet have obeyed the rules walk free?

Would we avoid the souls that are simply hungry for love and understanding?

Who would we elevate to lead our communities?

Which type of soul would win your heart?

Perhaps it is our current vision that is truly blind.

Blind to the soul that lies within the body.

Blind to the soul that lies behind the face.

HATE the HATE

ate seems to be getting a bad rap these days. I've seen sweatshirts and t-shirts with quips about how we need to rid the world of this age-old passion called hate.

Little sayings such as "Kindness Kills Hate," Or "Eliminate Hate," that adorn bumper stickers, t-shirts, and sweatshirts and are found on sidewalks and in coffee shops all about town. I even saw one recently that said: "I Hate Hate." To me, that was double-down stupid and I kind of hate it. It's a redundant oxymoron if you think about it. But please don't tell the hate haters that I hate it, or they might hate me.

I'm guessing if you stop one of the hate haters on the street and talk to them long enough you will find out that they do in fact hate a few things also. Like I'm guessing they might admit to hating hate. Which of course makes them hypocrites, but they would of course hate admitting or hearing that.

While I understand the motivation to eradicate the emotion of hate, I'm confident and comfortable enough with myself to state that I enjoy some hate on occasion.

For example, I hate coconut. And I kind of enjoy my hate of the stuff. The strange-tasting little fruit with the texture of eating a wax candle is worthy of my hate, I think, and I enjoy my hate, thank you very much.

Now I will tell you that I can't think of one person on the entire planet that I hate. However, I do hate many of the opinions of some people that I see or hear. Like the former esteemed leader of the House of Representatives, Nancy Pelosi. I didn't hate her. I hated her views and rhetoric, but who can hate an 81-year-old lady who went to work every day aboard her private jet? I admired her for being 81 and that she could get "whack-a-doodles" to listen to what she thinks. Even though I hated her positions, I didn't hate her.

Then at the other end of the age spectrum is AOC, or Alexandria Ocasio-Cortez. Did you know all you have to do is type AOC into Google and she pops up first and foremost with numerous entries! If you type my initials in Google—JGB—you get a mixed bag of entries from companies that sell industrial hoses to the Jerry Garcia Band. You never find little old me.

But getting back to AOC. I hate a lot of the stuff she stands for and that she says. And I sort of enjoy having hate for her bullshit. But I don't hate her. As a matter of fact, I think she is damn good-looking, and one must admire what she has pulled off to go from being a bartender to a powerful politician in Congress. So, no hate for her personally, just hatred for her lunacy.

To be honest, I'm comfortable with my hate for both Pelosi's and AOC's bullshit and I somewhat enjoy my hatred.

So, in my view—we don't need to eliminate hate. We just need to understand where it is best applied and where it should not be applied.

Hate for people—no, that is not needed and is uncalled for.

Hate for coconut is acceptable and understandable.

Hate for views, opinions, and policies of the coconuts such as Pelosi and AOC—again, acceptable and understandable.

But let it be fully understood, I don't hate anyone. Furthermore, I don't even hate hate.

Do What is Right

When conflict burns inside of you

and problems exist of what to do.

One directive can lead to resolve

the turmoil that bleeds until solved.

A lesson of the ages must always be in mind.

For it remains true to the test for all time.

It doesn't matter **_who_** is right.

The only thing that matters is **_what_** is right.

Stories

Everyone has a story.

A unique story.

Mine is unique to me and it's mine.

Yours is unique to you and only you.

Some are shared with a lot of others.

Some shared with very few.

Each story is noteworthy to those who lived it.

To those who didn't, many stories fall to insignificance.

But every story has value if allowed to be understood.

To have significance, the owner must permit the story to be told.

And the listener must be open to allow understanding.

When the message is permitted to run freely to the heart,

not slowed by the dams within the mind, understanding prevails.

There is an inherent dam lying between every mind and every heart.

Dams are built over time out of falsehoods, poor examples, and misunderstandings.

Tear down those dams of judgment. Let the story flow freely to your heart.

The story doesn't demand you agree; it simply yearns for you to better understand.

Time

Some have said, time is money. But it really isn't. Time is more valuable than money. Money we can make more of or get more of. But no matter how rich you are, time is something you can't make, get back, or get more of. Once the minute hand clicks forward, what's left behind is never coming back.

The days are long, but the years are short. While you're working the long hours, others are at home growing up. When they leave the nest, you will look back and think that time elapsed in the blink of an eye. It didn't. You were told exactly how long it would be, well in advance. You have known for years that there are twenty four hours in a day, seven days in a week, and 365 days in a year.

You have known since the day they were born when they will graduate high school. You know they will be going off to college, the military, or a job and you will be emptying the nest. You had plenty of warnings. You had choices. You still have choices. Money can't buy time or do-overs. The excuse that you didn't realize how fast time would fly by is nonsense. Of course, you knew.

When you have choices of where or with whom to spend your time, choose the ones you would want to be with if you only had one day left to live. 'Cause there ain't no guarantees they will be here tomorrow.

Today is yesterday's future.

Today is tomorrow's past.

Therefore, today is the only day you can live

in both the future and the past.

Today is the only day that is guaranteed.

Be present, today.

Today is the only day you can be present. There are no guarantees about being or getting to be present tomorrow. Just because you're confident you will be available tomorrow doesn't mean who you want to be with or what you want to do will be available.

If you knew you only had one more day to be on this earth, who would you want to spend it with?

Once the next minute or hour is spent, there are no rewinds. It's gone like dust in the wind.

Spend time wisely and use it in a way where you won't look back and wonder where it all went and wish you had spent your time differently.

Someone asked me once, "If you knew you only had a few days to live, who would you want to make amends with or see that you haven't seen in years?" After I thought about it for a couple of minutes, I had a couple of people in mind. My friend then asked me, "What's stopping you from contacting or seeing them now? There are no guarantees they will be around when you know your end is near. Maybe their end is near, and they don't have the ability to reach out.

Maybe your end will happen so suddenly you won't get notice or time to make the calls you want or need to make."

I soon realized that the only thing stopping me from reaching out now was me. Whether it was pride, ego, or just being lazy—I had a couple of calls to make and I did. Each call went far better than my imagination thought it would. I felt better and walked and slept just a little better, and a little lighter from then on. I was carrying less burdens and it reminded me of an age-old saying that is so true: "Forgiveness is a gift you give yourself."

We all make choices; every day we make several. One of the most critical choices you make every day is how you will be spending your time. Are you scheduling your life away from those you love? Are you spending time and energy avoiding people you need to build a bridge with? Make the right choices; choices you can live with if those you love, those you care about, those you miss and need to see again—are taken from you without notice.

The Path

Perfection, I have often said, is like a straight line. It is impossible to walk a perfectly straight path continuously. We will all deviate at times. The key, however, is to minimize the deviations or degree of deviation, and always try to be pointing your way back to the straight line.

This is true for your emotions, behavior, and attitude. Each has a path of perfection, but no one walks that line consistently. However, you can and should always be aiming for the pathway that is in balance. Don't let the deviations grow and expand.

What Makes a
Purposeful Life?

In my estimation, a purposeful life is one where activity and challenge exceed inaction and fear. Where friendship and love exceed loneliness and hate. Where hopes and dreams exceed doom and gloom.

But mostly, my life will be purposeful when my interaction with others leaves only positive influence.

Recycled Energy

I ask you to answer this only unto yourself.

Have you used the tragedies in your life as roadblocks or as propellants to a better you?

Facing issues and putting problems to sleep is usually not the easy way.

But it is always the better way.

If there is but one thing one must remember in order to lead a happy life, it is this.

No matter what life throws at you, good or bad, you must absorb it, then recycle it into energy from which to grow and move forward.

I think there are but two types of minds. Those that focus on being miserable and those that focus on being happy. Luckily, we have the option to choose and the ability to change.

Artificial Intelligence

Nothing works today without a PIN number, a security code, or a password.

I can't get a message, I can't get MY money, I can't get into my house or turn on my computer if I don't have that secret code.

Close doesn't count! I will try it again, X97T492. What do you mean, "unable to authorize access"? Should I try it again, or do I need help? Yeah, I need help—help from a hammer!

Where will it end? Will I someday need a password to say hello to my neighbor or a security code to have a dream? Or maybe I will need a PIN number to tie my shoes.

They call this Artificial Intelligence or AI.

Really? I have something else to call this nonsense.

Instead, how about P-I-T-A— or a genuine Pain in the Ass?

Dreams of Heaven

I know not what heaven shall look like nor feel like, but I do have a dream of how I wish it could be.

On earth, whenever my daughter thinks of me, an angel shall appear in her resemblance and shall place a loving kiss upon my cheek, then whisper gently in my ear, "I love you, Dad."

And if this dream of heaven could be true, nothing else would matter.

Rusty and Alive!

Please don't look upon me with pity-filled eyes.

For I still have a story to unload, and happily, I'm still alive!

I've had a good life even though in times past, I carried a heavy load.

I was blessed, whether carrying someone's garbage or someone's gold.

For me, life isn't about the weight or value of the haul.

No, life has been more about giving love and service to one and all.

Now, as you can obviously see, I can't carry as much as I once did.

And sadly, over time, I have even lost my lid!

It's true, I know; I no longer look nor work like I did back when.

But I still have a valuable story to tell, if you will listen to me now and then.

My inspiration for Rusty and Alive

Part Five

Essays

On occasion I get carried away on a subject and the result is more of an essay than a page or two of reflection. Some would call it rambling —I prefer to call it an essay.

A few of these pieces tackle particular subjects like socialism or problems we face. Others grew from stories I needed to retell, like "My Dad, My Dog, and The Mouse."

I've always enjoyed reading essays, particularly Ralph Waldo Emerson and Henry David Thoreau. I have no pretense that my writings approach the quality or consequence of either. But their work has influenced my thinking and, perhaps more importantly, my living.

I've found particular solace in one paragraph from Emerson's "Self-Reliance," written in 1841:

> *"If our young men miscarry in their first enterprises, they lose all heart. If the young merchant fails, men say he is ruined. If the finest genius studies at one of our colleges and is not*

installed in an office within one year afterwards in the cities or suburbs of Boston or New York, it seems to his friends and to himself that he is right in being disheartened, and in complaining the rest of his life. A sturdy lad from New Hampshire or Vermont, who in turn tries all the professions, who teams it, farms it, peddles, keeps a school, preaches, edits a newspaper, goes to Congress, buys a township, and so forth, in successive years, and always, like a cat, falls on his feet, is worth a hundred of these city dolls. He walks abreast with his days, and feels no shame in not 'studying a profession,' for he does not postpone his life, but lives already. He has not one chance, but a hundred chances."

I hope you enjoy my rambling essays.

My Dad, My Dog, and the Mouse

While it was almost forty years ago that it occurred, the story of my Dad, the Dog and the Mouse still ranks as one of the funniest things I have ever witnessed with my father. Let me tell you how it happened.

My family and I were living on a small acreage about two miles outside of town. We owned five acres, we had a horse named Cadet and a Golden Retriever named Brandy. Sundays were, and still remain, a ritual in our family where we all try to eat a meal together and catch up. This particular Sunday, we had invited my parents out to the acreage to grill some burgers for dinner.

Before dinner I asked Dad if he wanted to go with me out to the horse pasture as I needed to fix some fence at the far northern boundary of the property. Dad was very handy with tools and even more so with advice on how he thought I should be doing things, and always interested in anything I was up to. Dad was sixty years old at the time, very active and very hands-on with all projects.

On this particular Sunday, as we headed out towards the north fence line, my dog Brandy was not far behind and like your typical Golden Retriever she was working the grasses and brush to see what she could stir up. Dad and I were laughing at her and how she was going back and forth, nose to the ground, tail wagging 100 miles an hour with incredible enthusiasm that she might catch something. There was no doubt in her mind about the results. Brandy was the smartest, most intuitive dog I ever owned. Oh, how I miss that dog!

Cadet, my horse, was in the pasture. Cadet also was a very curious horse and would typically follow me around when I was in the field. But on this sunny afternoon, a fresh bale of hay thrown in his feed bunk earlier was a much higher priority than we humans with a dog trespassing in his pasture.

Dad and I could not have been more than about 200 feet out in the pasture when I spot a field mouse on the ground between Dad and myself. I stopped and quietly said to Dad as I pointed to the mouse, "Look, Dad, there is a little mouse rousing around in the grass—right there." After spotting the mouse, Dad turned slightly and called Brandy to come. Brandy lifted her head to see who and why someone was being so rude as to try to pull her off her hunt. I pat my leg a couple of times and said to her: "Brandy, come—Brandy, mouse!" and she headed our way in a full sprint.

The second she got within a foot or two she had her nose down and the little mouse took off to find a hiding place safe from Brandy's nose and paws. Suddenly, my Dad started kicking about like a wild man and screaming at a soprano pitch that I had never heard from him before.

"The mouse—the mouse—it went up my pant leg!" He raised one knee up then the other while standing in place and at the same time trying to grab his right leg. The mouse had apparently decided to seek refuge and had run up his shoe and into his pants.

At first I didn't know what to do and then my dad yelled at me in pure panic mode, "Get it, Jerry—get it out of my pants!"

I quickly dropped to my knees and grabbed Dad's right leg with both hands. Brandy was now barking wildly at all the excitement, but not sure what to do or what's going on. She was wildly circling us both trying to sniff out where that mouse went.

I slowly pulled my hands down his leg trying to act almost like a squeegee to force the mouse from his pants. As I got close to his ankles he said to me, "Okay, I think you got it."

"Dad, I didn't see it come out anywhere."

"No—but I think it's gone. I can't feel a thing."

I said, "Well, let me do that again from a different angle so we can make sure."

I grabbed his leg again but this time from his side and once again with a full hand wrap around his leg do the squeegee all way down to his foot. Again, he insisted it was gone. We both had a good laugh about it and by this time Brandy had calmed down and was off once again on her ever-enthusiastic hunt.

I picked my tools up and said to Dad with a wink and a smile: "Do you mind if we get to work now? I have to get this north fence repaired before dinner."

My father and I have always had a relationship where we tease each other and give each other crap whenever we can. It must run in the family because I have the same sort of relationship with both of my now adult daughters. We call it bantering or teasing. We tell our friends and others that we only tease the people we love or like.

Dad and I proceeded north. Brandy was trying to proceed northerly also, but her route was far more zigzag east to west, working the field as she slightly headed north with each east to west pass. Of course, being a dog, she was doing it at almost a full run and as a result pretty much keeping up with us as we made a direct line.

We reached the fence after about a five-minute walk. I put my tools down and I was beginning to gather up the broken strand of barbed wire when I suddenly heard from behind me: "Jerry—Jerry—the mouse, the mouse!" in that same shrill scream I had heard a few minutes earlier.

I turned around and I saw one of the funniest and craziest scenes I have ever witnessed regarding my dad. He was running away from me through the field as fast as his crazy condition will allow. His pants had slid down around his ankles, and his boxer shorts started to collapse to the degree where you might guess him to be a plumber. His hands flailed about, trying to slap his back, while he ran and screamed as though he was on fire.

I ran after him at full to catch him. Luckily, with his being in his sixties and me in my early thirties, but mostly because of the limits of his pants around his ankles, I caught him quickly. I grabbed him at his side and yelled, "Dad—hold still—where is it?"

Out of breath and in panic he said, "I think it went up under my shirt —get it, quick—get it!"

"Bend over and I'll get it out."

He leaned forward. I laid my arm full breadth across his back and again, trying to use my arm to act like a squeegee or broom, I slowly tried to work from his bottom up his back towards his neck. As I neared his shoulder blades, suddenly the mouse sprang out from under his shirt collar and ran to the bald spot on the back crest of his head.

The mouse stopped and looked around right to left and left to right as though trying to check traffic before crossing a busy street. It then suddenly jumped off and disappeared into the field never to be seen again.

I said, "I got him—he's gone."

"Are you sure? Maybe there was more than one?"

I dropped to the ground in laughter. Within a couple of seconds, I was laughing so hard my stomach was aching. Brandy was trying to lick my face in excitement as though she approved.

Dad was busy pulling up his pants, tucking in his shirt, fastening his belt and trying to catch his breath. Finally he said to me, "It isn't funny—the damn thing was in my crotch and then ran up my back."

I soon recovered. We quickly repaired the fence but I just couldn't stop laughing and my dad couldn't stop telling me it wasn't funny.

We went back to the house where my mom, wife, and kids were and of course I had to tell them of our encounter with the mouse and Dad's ensuing run through the field, pants around his ankles. I could hardly get it out through my laughter and tears as Dad sat red-faced, but smiling and giggling.

Dad is 99 now and doing great. I don't think he has the speed that he possessed back then and probably doesn't have either the agility or desire to run with his pants at his ankles through a field. But, without doubt, it was the funniest scene and memory I have with my Dad. In the end, I think the mouse won!

Unconditional
Love of Family

I will probably never forget one certain Sunday morning. My wife and I were in the car with our two girls in tow. We were headed out to breakfast, with no idea of where to go. We polled the girls, and each had different ideas which this Sunday morning was not in alignment with either Mom or Dad's ideas. My eldest daughter was probably ten or eleven years old, the little one around five to six years old.

As our Sunday journey headed nowhere, each girl started to become quite boisterous and competitive between each other as to where they either did or did not want to go. As parents, my wife and I always allowed our daughters to argue their case and learn to debate. We encouraged them to use their minds to further their argument versus volume but with children that concept didn't always work past the first or second rebuttal.

Now that they are adults and I have not only suffered through the teenage years but also still deal with their debating abilities as adults, I wonder sometimes, "What the hell were we thinking?" We blindly or stupidly felt the ability to debate would be used with or against others, such as boyfriends, spouses, and friends or more importantly against bad influences like boyfriends, spouses, or friends. With the aid of hindsight, I think I might do things a bit differently. Now it seems that the debating skills they have developed are more directed towards me. Well, maybe not just me, but their husbands and me.

As I was saying, on this particular Sunday, the girls were approximately ten and five years old. Oh, the good ol' days! You know, back in the day when if I said something it had meaning or had a far greater level of impact. Also interpreted as meaning they listened more so than they do today and they actually obeyed (for the most part).

Well, on this day, as the debate raged on in the back seat until I finally reached the point where I was done and Mom and Dad were going to make the executive decision of going where we wanted to go. It is interesting how these backseat debates can rage between two children and the parents can simultaneously carry on a low, calm and quiet conversation in the front seat as to what to do and where to go.

It's as though there is an invisible chauffeur's glass barrier between us. This makes obvious sense because in fact we are nothing more than chauffeurs. On this morning's journey, while the glass was up and the debate was at the screaming and nearing the hitting and kicking stage, Mom and I made an executive decision. We were going to go to the Garden Café, that's it, no discussion, no debate. Neither child had been pushing the Garden Café. Each had other ideas.

Lindsay, our youngest and being our conciliatory, peacemaker child, said "Okay, Dad, that's fine with me." Kelley, the elder, argue-with-a-wall child, who always had this underlying tone of "it's my way or I will kill you," daughter said "No, I don't want to go to the Garden Café. I hate that place and they don't have anything I like." Never mind that we went there numerous times in the past several months and she always ate well and didn't complain (for the most part). No, this morning she hated it and would not go there. She had made up her mind she was going to be mad.

As Lindsay settled into her regular routine of playing with her Pretty Little Ponies, singing and making conversation with them, Kelley bristled with anger and looked for reasons to be mad. You know, those major transgressions such as Lindsay's ponies invading the neutral zone of the back seat. World War III is about to erupt. Luckily for my wife and me, the drive to the Garden Café was short.

Once we parked the car and headed across the street to the restaurant, I pulled Kelley off to the side and asked her to be nice and tried to make a couple of goofy faces at her. With Kelley if I could get her to laugh, sometimes she would lighten up and move on. Not today. We were seated shortly with menus and out of the corner of my eye I see Kelley sitting in her chair, arms crossed, scowl pasted on with this "I'm mad as hell and I'm not taking this anymore" look on her face. The menu on the table closed and of no use other than to make a statement. I say to her "Kelley, pick something out to eat. They have lots of things you like such as waffles."

Kelley: "I hate waffles."

Dad: "No, you don't—you eat them at Grandma's all the time."

Kelley: "This isn't Grandma's."

Dad: "Kelley, you're acting like a big baby—you're going to eat. Now pick something out or I will pick something out for you."

Kelley: "I'm not eating."

Dad: "Kelley—this is your last warning. Either pick up the menu and pick something out or you're going to be in trouble with your father."

Kelley: "I don't care."

Okay—that does it! Let's go! I stand and pull her out of her chair and take her hand and say "You and I are going to the car." And to the car we go. Now, when Kelley was more like five to seven years old a spanking would have resulted from her attitude and mouth. Kelley was not a spankless child to say the least. At times I worried about how much I spanked her. I tried alternatives like taking things away, timeouts, talking, pleading, but never giving in or giving up. Somehow, somewhere, someday, I would win. Figuring out which one of us is more stubborn is best left to someone else.

Today she claims I'm more stubborn and I'm positive she is. But then, at ten or eleven years old I was trying to appeal to her mind and heart. Kelley was an incredibly intelligent girl. Perhaps she is too smart for her own good at times. And she was a very sweet loving girl. Even more so evident as she has become an adult, a wife, and now a mother. But when she was young, finding or getting to her heart was tougher than getting to her mind. She took incredible pride in being tough. I think or know that came from her training as a gymnast, but still, come on—she's a girl. There has to be a soft heart in there somewhere. Doesn't there? Let's not ask her sister that question—I think she may disagree.

As we sat in the car, of course my first dialogues started something like "What is your problem? I know you didn't want to come here, but you should respect your mother and father's decision." And then I probably broke into some or maybe I should say "another" long-winded, one-sided lecture. But this time, I struck upon a point that both Kelley and I would remember forever.

My point of unusual genius—"Why is it you would treat friends better than you would treat your loved ones or family?" I explained to Kelley that had she stayed overnight with her pal Ashley, and had Ashley's parents this morning taken them out to breakfast, and should her parents have decided to come to Garden Café, she would have smiled sweetly, said "no problem" and she would have eaten like we all know she is capable of. Most likely a waffle. But no, because she doesn't get her way with us, she proceeds to throw a tantrum and act like a little turd. (Turd is a technical term meaning person who is being a selfish jerk).

I lectured with uncommon genius, "She treats her friends and her friends' parents better than she treats her own parents and family." After a bit, we left the car and headed back to the restaurant and Kelley continued to be mad, but she ate a few bites of food as she knew that otherwise I would ground her from attending gymnastics. Her stubborn pride at the time would not allow her to admit to my genius of course, no way, that would show weakness. But years later she told me she recalled that incident and remembers even thinking "He's right." My redemption!

As some know, I tend to be agnostic. Meaning, I don't follow or belong to organized religions but do believe in God or a Superior Power. I won't go into that whole situation now but only bring it up to illustrate one point about my incident and ensuing lecture with Kelley. Long ago, I read in a book by Og Mandino that if anyone wonders if God is present or around all they have to do is look or listen for God's hand. God's hand often works through others in ways we don't often see or feel unless looking. For example, God obviously was influencing Abraham Lincoln's hands as he penned during his long ride the 272 words contained in the Gettysburg Address. And again, God's hand was evident in Martin Luther King Jr.'s address where he told the audience about his dream.

Listen to a song that brings you peace, or reminds you of someone you love and, in my view, God's hand was holding the author's pen. And in my view, there is little doubt that God holds a paintbrush, sculpts, influences numerous other great moments today and in history. Somewhere somehow, God planted a seed in my mind that day that ended up being translated into a lecture that would be remembered by both father and daughter to this day. God's influence was working that day on a short-tempered dad and a pig-headed daughter.

But allow me to return to my point. Why is it that we often treat our friends or even strangers better than we treat our loved ones? First of all, we don't think. We don't think about our trespasses and we don't think about how we might be hurting our loved ones. Secondly, in the midst of anger or coarse action there are very few that can stop and think about how our actions would be different if we were with friends versus family. As I said, we don't think.

But mostly, I have concluded that we act as we sometimes do because of our knowledge of the unconditional love that we have from our family and loved ones. We inherently know that we can be an ass with our parents, our sister, our husband, wife or other because our love and acceptance is never at risk. We know we have their unconditional love. We work at earning love and acceptance from friends, but with family? No, the love of family is taken for granted. Unfortunately, too often it is. Now, understanding this, when I'm on the receiving end of bad behavior gives me some comfort. I know what an incredible gift unconditional love is to give and to receive. It is just so precious a resource.

When my feelings are being trampled on by a loved one and feel that they are treating me worse than they would treat a friend, I try to stop and realize they are only doing so because they feel unconditional love from me and in turn, they also have unconditional love for me. It still stings a bit and perhaps they should be called out for their actions or words, but all with the basis of knowing our love for each other is without compromise or condition. Knowing we share this unconditional love brings me peace which helps heal the wounds. But also understand, our family and those we love unconditionally, are also our best friends, as we should try our best to treat them as such.

I Miss My Burn Barrel!

I'm guessing that a male invented foam peanuts. You know, those little foam, peanut-shaped thinga-ma-jigs they use to keep your fragilities safe when packed in a box? Unlike a man, a woman would have seen past their primary duty. Like what happens with these little pests after you remove the Christmas plate Aunt Matilda has sent? A woman would have thought of the mess they can make or the frustration to mankind that they can cause.

Today I was "preparing" the trash. Our trash pick-up day is tomorrow and in our new world of environmental concern we don't just take out the trash, but we have to "prepare" the trash prior to taking it to the curb. This new exercise in trash conscience or trash management might be in the best interest of our environment but still; prepare the trash? Is it all that much better of a system than when I was a kid in that small southwest Iowa town of Glenwood? Does it really help protect our environment? I care about our environment. I want a good clean world for my wasteful years. I mean really, when I'm to the point where I need someone to wipe the Jell-O from my chin, I don't want to look out the window of my nursing home and see nothing but plastic sacks stuck in my imaginary trees.

When I was a kid taking out the trash was fun! But it didn't require preparation, just a match and a barrel. I don't recall when I was finally old enough to take out the garbage my family produced. Most likely, I had followed my dad on other occasions and some night when he was working late it was suddenly decided I was old enough to handle such a dangerous mission on my own. The burn barrel was a big old rusted barrel located at the furthest point away from our house our yard would allow. Since we didn't have air conditioning and Iowa winds can change direction as fast as a teenage daughter changes her mood, keeping it away from the house was important.

Upon arrival to the barrel, I would dump the trash and quickly assess what was flammable and what was not. This is where a boy learns what will be later confirmed by schoolteachers about the physical properties of a variety of products. Such as paper burns faster than wood and that tin or glass are non-combustible. Once you dumped the trash in the barrel and assessed today's materials, then the fun began. I would take the matchbox from my pocket and pull out a match. At this point there is another important decision for a boy to make; does he strike the match on the strike plate of the matchbox or does he give it a try on the zipper of his jeans like cowboys do? Is anyone watching?

To get a good trash fire it may take several matches and stacking of the paper or cardboard. Maybe a torch is better? Just hold about five or six matches together when lighting and *sha-bam!* you've got a torch. Empty Frosted Flakes boxes make for a good burn and also act like a chimney. There is just something incredibly mesmerizing about watching Tony the Tiger burn while standing on his head.

Once the fire was going well I could then switch gears to my next fire adventure. Take a stick and start churning up the old trash from previous fires to see what kind of expanded fire one could get and how deep into the barrel you could generate new flames. Now how cool is that? But I digress...

As I said earlier, in today's world we must "prepare" the trash. No dumping it all in the burn barrel and burning it all up. No, that's too easy. The trash has to be separated into various forms of recyclables. Here in Council Bluffs, glass goes into one tub, paper another, plastic or cans another. Is it #2 plastic or #5 plastic? Yes, to one, no to the other! And then, there are boxes. Our trash hauler demands that boxes over two cubic feet be flattened and put under the recycling tubs in a neat pile. Being the one who "prepares" the trash, breaking the boxes down is my job. I wonder if our trash hauler carries a cubic tape measure. I can just see them standing curbside with a measuring tape and a calculator determining which dismantled box goes and which one stays. It seems like at least once a month we have boxes. Why? I don't know—they just magically appear near the recycling tubs. Who buys stuff that needs a box? I guess we are on a mission to fill all the closets so someday we can have a garage sale in order to meet our neighbors.

I pick up a box and what do I see but those dreaded little foam peanuts. This over-the-size limit box is over half full of 'em. Now being an experienced box breaker and trash preparation engineer, I know what a pain these rascals can be. Thus, I think to myself "Be careful, these little bastards fly without notice and can be a pain, so take your time and devise a plan." I then realize I'm standing near my open garage door and the trash container is only about ten feet away. Our recycler doesn't take foam so they belong in the regular trash. I know what I will do, I will close the lid to the box, walk the ten feet to the trash container with one hand firmly on the lid of the box and then very carefully empty those little foam Jimmy Carters into the container and quickly close the lid. No sudden burst of wind is going to get me!

So off I go on my ten-foot expedition to contain the dreaded peanuts. I get to the trash container, flip open its lid and move to a position to help block any wind. I then lower the box into the container about midway. I open the box so I can dump the peanuts and lo and behold they are gone! No peanuts—but how? What happened? And then I see it—a large gap in the bottom of the box where the box flaps do not overlap and cause a generous breach. *Oh no!* I turn and what do I see —you got it—foam peanuts flying all over my driveway. $#!@*%!

I quickly turn and run for a broom and dustpan. I'm gathering them up as fast as I can but those little frustrates have wings or something. And every time I try to get them to the trash container, the wind takes most of them off my pan and into another world—such as the rose bushes next to the trash container zone. This is worse than trying to put socks on a rooster! I spend over ten minutes chasing foam peanuts. I have injuries from evacuating them from my rose bushes. I'm giving blood for this! Will there be scars from the foam war? Oh, how I hate these things.

I wonder about how much we are saving the environment with all this recycling. Now two diesel burning trucks come to get our trash. One for the normal trash another for the recyclables. Plastic tubs, plastic bags, wire ties, compactors, more trash trucks, more trash separators, more conveyor belts, hydraulic hoses, this, that and more. All this machinery, diesel trucks, recycling centers, etc. just to replace the old burn barrel in the back yard—really? All the while the world is still dealing with foam peanuts. And they call this progress?

Oh, how I miss my burn barrel!

The Super Seven!

A Fresh and Consolidated Version of "The Ten Commandments"

In my view, "The Ten Commandments" brought down from the mountain by Moses and written on stone tablets are just a bit outdated. For today's world I think we need to revisit the Commandments and see if we can make a few tweaks and still end up with some good rules to live by. I also think that Old Moses may have predetermined in his own mind that it had to be ten. Why not eight? Why not seven? I mean really, a couple of the commandments are somewhat redundant or could be condensed into one.

To help some of you heathens out there, let's revisit the original ten.

1. You shall have no other gods before Me.
2. You shall not make idols.
3. You shall not take the name of the LORD your God in vain.
4. Remember the Sabbath day, and keep it holy.
5. Honor your father and your mother.
6. You shall not murder.
7. You shall not commit adultery.
8. You shall not steal.

9. You shall not bear false witness against your neighbor.
10. You shall not covet.

1. You shall have no other gods before me.

This is outdated. I mean really. Does it matter who is first? Can't you have had a different God earlier and then switch? Don't we give out participation trophies now and skip the whole first, second, and third ranks?

2. You shall not make idols.

Outdated. What about American Idol? Go tell that to Carrie Underwood, and what's wrong with having an idol? I hope and aspire to be someone's idol! Obviously, I think the young person at the gym probably thinks of me as an idol but is just too shy to say it. Let's not condemn them to hell for it! Please!

3. You shall not take the name of the LORD your God in vain.

Again, this is so outdated. People have done it for hundreds of years and there is not one recorded incident in history where someone was struck by lightning. I can say "God dammit" a thousand times and what is going to happen? Rules without consequences are worthless.

4. Remember the Sabbath day, and keep it holy.

There is nothing wrong with working on Sunday. Who would make me a triple venti, skinny vanilla latte if it weren't for people working on Sunday? How would I get my honey-do list done? Home Depot would be closed? There is nothing wrong with hard work and we should encourage it. Hell, some have taken this outdated commandment so far as they think the Sabbath is every day of the week. They call it welfare. We need commandment reform.

5. Honor your father and your mother.

This is out and has to be gone. I'm sorry, but some fathers and mothers don't deserve to be honored. Apparently in Moses's day they didn't have deadbeat parents. Notice I didn't say Deadbeat Dads. That's because there are a lot of Deadbeat Moms in the world too!

6. You shall not murder.

Oh really? We need a commandment to tell us this? How has it worked thus far? The religious crusades—what about those? Wasn't there a lot of murdering going on in the name of God or Religion? Why do Commandments need to cover the same territory that laws cover?

7. You shall not commit adultery.

Okay. This one is okay, but can't we just group this in with the next two: thou shall not steal and thou shall not bear false witness? Do we really need three separate commandments for these three? And why do all these have to start with a negative? Thou shall not!!! Can't we give a positive commandment? How about to cover these three, we just simply say Thou Shall Be Honest and Tell the Truth. Doesn't that cover all three? If you're honest and always tell the truth you won't be committing adultery, you won't be stealing, and you won't bear false witness.

8. You shall not steal.

Gone!

9. You shall not bear false witness against your neighbor.

Gone and Delete!

10. You shall not covet thy neighbor's goods.

This one is also known as thou shall not covet thy neighbor's wife. Okay, I take exception to this one. I see nothing wrong with coveting my neighbor's stuff. It inspires me to work harder and for goodness sake this is what makes our economy work. Did Moses ever hear of Capitalism? It keeps the world going and prevents us from all killing one another. I mean really, if people weren't busy making and selling shit to fill other people's closets the world would disintegrate into mass chaos in days.

Secondly, in my own personal world, I have no issue agreeing not to covet my neighbor's wife. I have about five neighbors and I can guarantee you with 100% certainty I have zero interest in any of them.

Now, I will also admit that I do covet a couple of my buddies' wives. Nothing wrong with that! They are hot! But, coveting and going after are two totally different things. You shouldn't condemn me to hell for thinking my buddy is one lucky dude because his wife has a great body. But I think we can cover this topic a lot more simply. Let's change this commandment to something like "Thou shall not do anything illegal or immoral about your covets." Which in reality is also covered by agreeing to my earlier commandment about being honest and telling the truth. 'Cause if you are going to abide by that one, no way are you going to try to get your neighbor's wife into the sack or try to steal his brand new three-burner gas grill with attached smoker. So, I'm calling for complete elimination.

Here are my new and updated recommended commandments: I think these cover all the bases of living properly and are a lot more succinct and updated for today's world. Matter of fact, I don't think we will etch them in stone. Nope, we will put them on Facebook or X where everything lives into infinity.

1. Thou shall always use good manners.

I think if we all used good manners more consistently, a lot of other bad crap would go away. If we could all say please and thank you, or you're welcome more, far fewer people would get pissed off as much as they do. How about saying "excuse me" more or "I'm sorry" more. And, if everyone would abide by this commandment, road rage totally disappears.

2. You shall treat ALL others with respect and dignity.

If this happened consistently, almost all wars would end, most fights would not occur, people wouldn't get their feelings hurt, and good shit would happen. Hell, a lot of the political leadership folks would have nothing to bitch about and we might get something done in Congress too. This also earns an assist in elimination of Thou Shall not Covet thy neighbor's shit and wife. It would not be respectful to be chasing your neighbor's wife nor stealing his grill. Depending upon what state you live in, I'm not sure which of those two is a worse offense.

3. You shall always be honest and tell the truth.

This one takes care of three of our old, outdated commandments in one fell swoop. It replaces: thou shall not steal, thou shall not bear false witness, and thou shall not commit adultery. And it is much like the KISS method. Just keep it simple, stupid.

4. You shall always seek more knowledge.

The smarter we are or everyone becomes the less bad shit happens. A really smart person doesn't hold up a 7-Eleven. Case made and closed.

5. You shall be thankful for all your blessings.

This also helps reduce the coveting of your neighbor's shit! When one is thankful for what you already have, you feel better and you don't steal shit.

6. You shall respect and protect nature.

Okay, I'm throwing a bone to the environmentalists here. But also, I hate and despise litter. In my view any asshole who knowingly throws his McDonald's sack of trash out the window of his rusted-out Ford Taurus should be sent away to life in prison. I mean really. Anyone with that mentality has to have pig shit for brains and be a slime ball.

I'll bet the dude or dude-ette (I believe in equality here—don't want to leave out the women—God forbid) doesn't have a job and beats his or her spouse also. And furthermore, do we want this fine specimen being an example to its mentally challenged offspring? They already have enough issues to deal with—they don't need this quarter wit as life's example of a parent. I say no—send them away and lock 'em up forever.

7. You shall love and protect your country along with our Constitution and Bill of Rights.

Why? Because I said so. Since I'm playing the updated role of Moses here, I get at least one gimme.

There it is! "The Ten Commandments" are out and replaced with the Super Seven. Sounds like a drink at 7-Eleven, doesn't it? Stop by and get your Super Seven for only 49 cents while supplies last!

The Super Seven:

1. Thou shall always use good manners.
2. You shall treat ALL others with respect and dignity.
3. You shall always be honest and tell the truth.
4. You shall always seek more knowledge.
5. You shall be thankful for all your blessings.
6. You shall respect and protect nature.
7. You shall love and protect your country along with our Constitution and Bill of Rights.

Problems: Poison or Gold?

I t occurred to me the other day that problems, and one's ability to deal with them, can be one's gold or one's poison. In all realms of life, dealing with problems, issues, strife, challenges, calamities, setbacks, or failure creates pathways to the future.

We all universally know that if someone invents something that cures or fixes a problem, one can become rich! Start a business which helps resolve problems and others will beat a path to your door.

But problem solving also creates wealth on an individual basis in ways we don't often consider. Seldom do we think of wealth in terms of respect or leadership. However, one who has the respect of others and is looked to as a leader by their peers has great personal capital.

For example, think of a high school football player who can solve the problem of the opposing team moving at will down the field. The coach puts him in the game and, using both his physical and leadership skills, he directs and motivates others while performing at his personal best in order to bring about turnovers. In so doing he grows in personal wealth as his self-respect and the respect and admiration of his teammates, coaches, and fans grow. But what was the catalyst to this growth? A problem! Had a problem never presented itself, this skill, talent, and growth may never have had the opportunity to be exposed.

Think of two employees in the same company. Let's name them Betty and Bob. Both have the same relative skills, education, and experience. However, Bob has issues dealing with problems. Betty, on the other hand, is a problem solver. She sees issues or challenges and starts thinking of solutions. Bob, on the other hand, sees a problem and needs to go ask for direction or becomes handicapped. Often it is Betty offering Bob ideas or suggestions.

Bob goes home at night frustrated and depressed over his work problems and his lack of respect or promotion within the company. Betty, on the other hand, goes home at night energized by the challenges that are in front of her. She dreams and thinks of resolutions and can't wait to test them.

Which of the two will climb the corporate ladder faster? Which of these would you rather work with as an associate? Which of the two gets larger raises more often? Betty, of course, is our success example, but what again is interesting is that her gold is born out of problems! If there were no problems or challenges, Betty wouldn't have the opportunity to shine. It is through her attitude of acceptance of challenge, responsibility, and problems that creates her own wealth in terms of growth, respect, and earnings. Problems are Betty's gold.

On the other hand, problems are Bob's poison. They hinder him financially and drain him emotionally. If Bob could learn to welcome problems, to understand their value, and to see the reward in overcoming them, he could eventually turn poison to gold.

People who accept problems as challenges and opportunity are generally happier and more successful. People, teams, organizations, communities, and corporations seek problem solvers out and often call them leaders.

Let's look at another instance where problems exist and how they are handled. Problems within families. There is not a family where problems of one sort or another don't occur.

However, it is the family's ability to accept and deal with its problems that ultimately determines the family's happiness, wellbeing, and that of all of its members. M. Scott Peck wrote in the book *The Road Less Traveled* that understanding and accepting the fact that life is difficult and wrought with hurdles is the beginning of finding happiness. If we live with an expectation of a problem-free life, then the smallest of problems explodes with negativity beyond its true warrant.

Whereas the family that knows how to absorb and absolve its problems is a family that does well. They understand that problems are a part of everyday life. The parents' attitude and leadership in this is key.

Further, an attitude taught by example to children that problems are to be expected and not dramatized, sets the child up for success as an adult. Helping children understand the need and the rewards that come from solving their own problems, or being a problem solver, is a key to happiness as an adult.

In the end, whether it be on a personal level, a business level, or throughout life, we need to understand that with problems comes opportunity and choice. Each person is presented with problems, and when so presented, it comes time for a choice. A choice as to how we will deal with the problem before us. Will the problems before us turn into a piece of gold or will we allow them to become a poison within our ranks? Will I be a problem solver or a problem avoider?

We all lead by example, whether it be a positive or poor one—an example it is.

Thus, I challenge you: rejoice in your problems! They are your gold if you use them properly and carry the right attitude toward them. They only become your poison when you allow them to overtake you or to be used as excuses.

> *"Problems are to the mind what exercise is to the muscles, they toughen and make strong."*

—Norman Vincent Peale

Thoughts on Socialism

Socialism is the universal leveling of the playing field. It may sound good in platitudes of fairness, equity, and so on, but unfortunately, nice platitudes seldom have a thing to do with reality.

Fairness for all is the goal of those who lack the vision, energy, ambition, and drive to earn for themselves that which they believe should be given to them without effort. Thus, in truth, jealousy or envy is the basis and foundation of socialism.

Socialism only works until you run out of other people's money.

Socialism is based upon equality. Equality in suffering. Equality in scarcity. Equality in squalor. It is not about raising others up, it is about bringing down those who work hard and achieve. It is about putting a cap on achievement and success.

Socialism is the elimination of hopes, dreams, aspirations, drive, uniqueness, ambition, and achievement. It is the glorification of sameness, weakness of thought, the loss of effort and ambition, and the sterilization of creativity.

Socialism doesn't flatten or level power amongst all. It focuses power more finitely directly to those who are the collectors and redistributors—government leadership. Every socialist leader in history died incredibly rich or lived in great splendor while their people suffered immensely. Hitler, Castro, Chavez, Marx, Lenin, Mao, and more.

Power and wealth are more widely distributed in a capitalistic democracy than they are in a socialistic society. A broader number of people with diverse views and abilities have so-called power and wealth in a capitalistic democracy. Whereas very few, only political leaders, have the power and wealth in a socialistic society.

To be a socialist, you must put aside long-term logical thinking and must adopt a short-term, lazy, selfish ideology.

Successful Socialism is the ultimate oxymoron. In socialism—success is penalized.

One who aspires to be a leader in a socialistic system is saying to you they want to be the one who is the collector and redistributor of everyone else's money and possessions. In so doing, they get to ensure their life is just a little bit (or a lot) better than everyone else's. They get to be the decision-maker on who gets what and how much. But they sell it as equality. Show me a socialist leader who actually lived like the rest of his flock.

Why is it that underground black markets explode and thrive in socialist countries? It's a proven fact that socialism promotes corruption at far faster and deeper rates than capitalism or democracy.

In socialism, the primary theory is that you take from the rich and you give to the poor. What happens when there are no rich left to take from?

Winston Churchill said: "Socialism is a philosophy of failure, the creed of ignorance, and the gospel of envy; its inherent virtue is the equal sharing of misery."

He also said: "The inherent vice of capitalism is the unequal sharing of blessings; the inherent virtue of socialism is the equal sharing of miseries."

Ben Shapiro said: "Socialism states that you owe me simply because I exist. Capitalism, by contrast, results in a sort of reality-forced altruism: I may not want to help you, I may dislike you, but if I don't give you a product or service you want, I will starve. Voluntary exchange is moral redistribution. Socialism—or forced redistribution—is immoral."

"The American Republic will endure until the day Congress discovers that it can bribe the public with the public's money."

—Alexis de Tocqueville

"It's not an endlessly expanding list of rights—the 'right' to education, the 'right' to health care, the 'right' to food and housing. That's not freedom, that's dependency. Those aren't rights, those are the rations of slavery—hay and a barn for human cattle."

—Alexis de Tocqueville

"It is indeed difficult to imagine how men who have entirely renounced the habit of managing their own affairs could be successful in choosing those who ought to lead them. It is impossible to believe that a liberal, energetic, and wise government can ever emerge from the ballots of a nation of servants."

—Alexis de Tocqueville

"I hope we once again have reminded people that man is not free unless government is limited. There's a clear cause and effect here that is as neat and predictable as a law of physics: As government expands, liberty contracts."

—Ronald Reagan

"Government is not a solution to our problem; government is the problem."

—Ronald Reagan

The Freedom of Thought

I t's no secret or revelation that in today's America there is a great divide or polarization between opposing sides in the world of politics and political beliefs. I'm amongst those who feel my beliefs are superior and that everyone should see the world as I do. Obviously, the world would be a far better place if everyone would just agree with me and see things as I see them. But I'm also not so naïve as to believe that this will occur. I also have to allow for the possibility, however slight, that maybe I'm the one who is wrong.

However, what I will preach, lecture, write upon, and pontificate about with all the energy I can muster is that the solution to much of our divide is to encourage, among all people, respect for the Freedom of Thought.

Unlike Freedom of Speech or Freedom of Religion, the Freedom of Thought was not mentioned in the US Constitution or the Bill of Rights. But, it is implied through connection to the freedom of speech and freedom of religion as you can't act upon either speech or religion without thoughts on the subject at hand.

The Freedom of Thought is the genesis or beginning of what you might express with your constitutionally protected freedom of speech. And obviously, your constitutionally protected freedom of religion also begins with your personal freedom of thought.

Thus, how or what anyone believes is deserving of respect just as much as their freedom to speak on the issues or to worship as they please. Unfortunately, in today's societal environment all three are under attack from all sides. The political left and the political right are both disrespectful of the opposite side's rights to think or speak a differing opinion.

Sadly, those on the right or conservative side pass judgement on those on the left or liberal side by what we see in the far left fringe. For example, maybe the far left liberal 10% is how the left is judged by the conservatives. The conservatives lump them all into one basket. Likewise, the left judges and concludes that all conservatives are identical to the far right 10% of the conservative field. Both are wrong.

Probably 80% of the population leans one direction or the other and isn't as ardent and off the charts to the left or right as many would believe. It is those in this 80% (or so) middle that we must appeal to for some common-sense rationale.

To start with, we need to all have far more respect for the Freedom of Thought. We must respect that others are allowed and encouraged to see things differently than we do. Their so doing doesn't automatically make them wrong or dumb, or un-American, or as I like to say "wack-a-doodles." For explanation, a wack-a-doodle is a technical term that applies to the 10% fringe group from either side. They are deemed to just be "wacky" and therefore a "wack-a-doodle."

When we see people from the opposite side of our beliefs we need to realize that if we had lived their life, grew up when and where they grew up, read what they read, and lived the lives they have lived, we would most likely see things the same way they do.

We need to respect their freedom of thought. They deserve the same respect as we hope to receive. If we want those on the opposite side to respect our freedom of thought, then we need to respect theirs.

One can find writings or quotes on the Freedom of Thought throughout history. In ancient Greece, the fifth century BC, the principles of intellectual freedom were presented along with democratic ideals. They were later refined by great philosophers such as Socrates and Plato.

Throughout history, philosophers have continued to herald the principle in the writings of John Locke, Montaigne, and Voltaire. It raised its beautiful head again when Thomas Jefferson penned the Declaration of Independence and it was enshrined by our Founding Fathers in the US Constitution, First Amendment.

Freedom of Thought is not a new concept or belief. However, it is under attack and not just by those who are on the opposite side of your opinion. It may even be under attack or at minimum disregarded too often by you and me. When we fail to respect the right of others to see things differently than we do, then we too are part of the problem.

This isn't to say we can't disagree. But it is to say we owe respect to those whom we disagree with. For they deserve the freedom to think as they wish, just as we do.

We can disagree, but we don't need to be disagreeable or disrespectful.

> *"I disapprove of what you say, but I will defend to the death your right to say it."*
>
> —S.G. Tallentyre, The Friends of Voltaire

"Dare to think for yourself."

—Voltaire

"New opinions are always suspected, and usually opposed, without any other reason but because they are not already common."

—John Locke

"If you want to be wrong, then follow the masses."

—Socrates

"To find yourself, think for yourself."

—Plato

Something is Going on Here!

The Message of the Red-Winged Blackbird

I must admit that the day the red-winged blackbird delivered a message to me, I totally missed it. My mind wasn't looking for signs or messages. I was consumed with other mental entanglements like trying to get to an appointment, filling my car with gas, and worrying about my father.

But that pesky little bird was doing its utmost to get my attention to deliver its spiritual message. I wish the message would have clicked with me that morning but I can't change the past. As usual, all I can do is reflect upon it as I so often do. I will try to connect the dots of the series of events in a backward sequence to help make sense of it all.

In the fall of 2022 I was on a flight from Omaha to Phoenix. Bored, I started deleting old videos from my phone when I came across one that I instantly remembered.

I had been to my parents' assisted living apartment to check on them, but mainly my father. He was now in hospice care within their living unit and was not doing well. I had been there the night before and wanted to stop by again this morning to check on him and Mom and to see if there was anything I could do to benefit their comfort. Mom was fine and happy to see me. Dad was pretty much out of it as he lay in his bed. He would on occasion mumble or open his eyes, but that was the extent of any communications.

The hospice nurse suggested I go about my day—he didn't think Dad would pass today. I left for my office, stopping at a gas station on the way.

As soon as I parked the car under the gas station canopy a red-winged blackbird landed on my passenger-side external mirror. It then hopped to the window edge and would switch its gaze between the mirror and me sitting in the driver's seat. Then, it would hop back to the top of the mirror, wings fluttering and sit and stare at me. I thought to myself, "You crazy bird—what is your problem?" This went on for a couple of minutes, and realizing I was more intrigued by this bird than in a hurry to get gas, I sat and watched for a bit.

After a while I decided enough is enough and I proceeded to get out of the car and start pumping gas. But little red-winged blackbird continued with his fluttering back and forth between the mirror and the window ledge. After filling the car, I proceeded to get back inside and sure enough Mr. Persistent Bird was still there and acting the same.

I thought to myself, my grandkids would get a kick out of this so I reached for my iPhone and started recording a video of this goofball bird entranced with my car window and mirror. After 36 seconds of video I felt I had adequate evidence to show the kids so I put the car in drive and began my exit. The bird tried to keep up with the car for a second or two but obviously couldn't and we parted ways.

After recalling all the odd details of the encounter that day, sitting mid-flight, I was about to delete the video from my phone when for some odd reason I noted the time and date the video was shot: 9:39

a.m. June 1, 2022. The date struck me. Wait a minute I thought, isn't that the date Dad passed away? I knew it was but needed to verify and went to my calendar and verified that sure enough Dad had died that very same day at about 3:30pm. While the hospice nurse just that morning felt Dad wouldn't pass that day, things progressed rapidly and I was called back to his bedside at about noon that day.

As the flight continued, I reflected upon the red-winged blackbird being on my window that same morning my dad passed away and I then recalled that my Dad had a somewhat love-hate relationship with red-winged blackbirds.

Dad loved to mow at my farm. It was his favorite thing to do until he was about 98 years old and his failing balance and agility had forced me to shut that activity off before he got seriously hurt. He would drive to the farm and get on the riding mower and mow for one to three hours almost every day by himself. One day he had fallen trying to get on the mower and lay there, unable to get up for over an hour until he used his cell phone to call one of our neighbors. That was the end of his mowing and he was not happy with me over it.

He would often tell me about his mowing and if he had seen any deer or turkey or complain that the mower needed this or that and I needed to get on it before his next mowing. One common topic was his talking about those pesky red-winged blackbirds. As he would mow by the marshes or streams they would dive-bomb around him. Sometimes he felt they were going to hit him in the face or head. At other times he felt they were amazing to watch. He didn't know if they were attacking flying bugs his mower had stirred up or if they were trying to dissuade him from being so close to their nests in the marsh areas. Either way, he couldn't get over how close they came to him and was amazed at their agility.

After departing the flight and airport I continued on to my Arizona home and just couldn't get this weird connection of the red-winged blackbird being on my window the very morning of my Dad's death and the additional connection of Dad's blackbird encounters being a consistent topic in our past.

I felt as though, "Something is going on here."

I'm a big believer in the spiritual world, and nothing is an accident or a simple coincidence. I believe people cross paths for a reason. We don't always know why, and we often miss the opportunity or message that is present in what may appear as a simple coincidence. This one, I couldn't let go of. But was I going down a rabbit hole with an incident in search of a meaning?

With the heavy feeling still on my mind, later that evening I sat on the back patio of my Arizona home, and I recall the full moon rising over the large cactus just outside the fence of my yard. It was a night worthy of reflection and thought.

As I sat with my Jack Daniels on ice I remembered I had read a book recently about the lore of the Lakota Indians and their spiritual beliefs. The Lakota had once occupied the general vicinity of my farm and I enjoyed learning about them. Not unlike a lot of native tribes, a lot of their beliefs are rooted in nature including trees, animals, the moon and stars. The overall message of the book was that when events occur in your life that seem to be interconnected, don't dismiss them and maybe, just maybe something spiritual is going on there.

As I sat there enjoying the starlit nightscape, I did the counterintuitive thing to do and I reached out to Google via my iPhone to research the Lakota Indians' spiritual meaning of a red-winged blackbird.

Here is what I found: it represents positive change, personal growth, and the ability to navigate life transitions while often serving as a guide to inner wisdom.

The dots were now connected. In my mind, the morning of June 1, 2022 a red-winged blackbird was attempting to deliver to me a warning message. The message being that later that day change would be coming. That I would grow from the change. That I would have to navigate life without my much-loved father and friend. That a transition was coming. I believe it was attempting to give me notice to prepare myself for the transition and life-altering change.

I'm okay with not understanding the message that very day. I got it and now get it. Better late than never. Red-winged blackbirds will never be taken for granted again by this humble servant.

Sometimes we all need to understand, accept and pay close attention when: "Something is going on here."

Acknowledgments

First off, I hope you have found something between the covers of this book that you enjoyed, made you think, or that resonated with you. If you did, my goal in sharing my writings in a published book has been accomplished.

Since I began writing back in May of 1995, I never wrote one piece with the intent of having an audience or for it to be shared. For years, I kept my writings, mostly done on yellow pad stuffed in a 3-ring binder, literally in my bedroom closet. On rare occasions I might share a writing or two with my daughters or a very, very close friend. The ego is a funny thing and we all have one. Ego's can push us or restrain us. When it came to my writings, my ego restrained me from sharing them outside of those with whom I felt a two-way unconditional love.

My male ego kept telling me that if I shared these writings, I might lose my man card or that some might rightfully judge me as being nuts. With time, maturity and a diminishing ego, I started sharing them with more and more people. My writings literally came out of the closet so to speak. The encouragement from close friends to publish or distribute them grew. But were they just telling me what they thought I wanted to hear? Their consistent push gave me the impetus to explore the potential.

Mark and Renee—Thank you!

When I wrote my first book, *Eat Sh*t and Smile: Surviving and Thriving on the Roller Coaster of Life* I had the good fortune to be paired with an editor out of Denver, Colorado by the name of James Thole of Story Gold Media.

Well after the book was published we had a phone conversation one day about the audio version of that book and I told James about my collection of writings, and that I was contemplating putting them together into some sort of book. James asked me to send him a few of my favorites for him to review and he would give me his thoughts. James is a great editor, writer, and publisher. I think he may also be a good salesman, or at minimum a promoter of people such as me, in publishing their musings. With his encouragement I sent him everything you see in this book and together we worked to bring *The Long Game* to reality. He helped me to reach a new goal which is to leave a bit of myself for my current and future generations of family. I can't thank James enough for his professional advice, edits, encouragement, and his very kind words throughout this process.

Thank you James!

For my final words of advice to my friends, family and readers, I will go back to the words of my father upon his 100th birthday.

Live everyday with love in your heart!

Jerry